THE DOCK BRIEF

WHAT SHALL WE TELL CAROLINE?

I SPY

Three Plays by

JOHN MORTIMER

THE DOCK BRIEF

WHAT SHALL WE TELL CAROLINE?

I SPY

GROVE PRESS, INC.   NEW YORK

CONTENTS

PREFACE

About three years ago Nesta Pain, whom I knew and admired as one of the most distinguished of radio producers, asked me to write a play for her. At that time I considered myself a novelist. It is true that during a lonely childhood I quite often acted through Hamlet *or* Macbeth *to the boredom of my parents, duelling with myself, quarrelling with myself, fooling myself I was mad for hours on end (it may be that this is why I was content not to see either of these masterpieces again for a very long time). It is also true that I spent several formative years in the documentary film world, eventually working as a script-writer; however, as most of my film life was spent making tea or playing pontoon with the electricians, and as, in my considered opinion, documentary films bear as little relation to art as they do to life, existing uninterestingly between the two like the instructions you get with do-it-yourself garden furniture, I was in no way prepared for the pleasures and excitements I have gained by accepting Nesta Pain's proposition. Indeed I put it off for a considerable time, even though she took me out to lunch and telephoned frequently. I am grateful now to her persistence.*

In the course of time THE DOCK BRIEF *occurred to me as an idea, and remembering Nesta Pain and her generosity over lunch I wrote it as a play. As I started to write I discovered I was writing with enormous enjoyment, in fact with such pleasure that I had difficulty, on buses or tube trains, in resisting the temptation to bring out a note book and do another page of dialogue. I had the uneasy*

7

suspicion that at last I was writing what I had wanted, all my life, to say. When asked what I was working on I used to say a play about two elderly men in a cell, this was always greeted with sympathetic pity: particularly by people who knew about the theatre.

We recorded THE DOCK BRIEF *first on a Sunday afternoon in a very small broadcasting studio while, in the outside emptiness, hymns boomed from the amplified church in Portland Place. I sat in the little fish tank and watched through the plate glass while two extremely accomplished actors spoke the lines with clear and gratifying enjoyment. I heard them with a wholly new sense of exhilaration. The writer of fiction writes dialogue for the mind and the eye, he uses blank paper in the same way as a dramatist uses silence. To write for the mind and the ear seems now to me far more exciting, and I cannot imagine writing except for words to be spoken.*

As a radio play THE DOCK BRIEF *had some success; it won the Italia Prize for radio and has been broadcast in a number of languages. I do not think that radio drama has achieved any particular status as an art, nor do I think it will survive, as a dramatic medium, against the competition of television, except for the performance of long and rarely done costume dramas of operatic dimensions where words are all important. Writing for radio has, as a technique however, its own fascination. On the whole a radio play appeals to an audience of thousands of individuals. A film or a play communicates with a crowd who can, with luck, give to each other, exchanging laughter and tears. A radio play speaks to a single listener and is at the mercy of his desire, frequently irresistible, to switch it off.*

This is what gives to radio its intimacy; it is reading to a blind man, or telling a story to a child in a darkened room. It is a conversation, whispered over the telephone, overheard, as on a crossed line, by thousands. It speaks confidentially into the earphones of the hospital patient, or murmurs from the battery set among the crumpled stockings

8

and photographs in the bedroom of a young girl who has nothing better to do than listen to it, and who has no desire to go downstairs and join the family circle.

To say this is not in any way to suggest that there is a hidden mystery in writing for radio. I do not think there is any great mystery in the mediums which are now open to a dramatic writer. The greatest danger for any writer is to get stuck with the idea of "pure radio" or "perfect television" or "pure cinema": the worship of a medium for its own sake has become the sign of a dramatic technique in search of an idea. The truth is that what matters is not cutting or camera angles or sound values or any special technique; but the communication by a writer who has something to say. In all its changes of medium, radio, television and the stage, THE DOCK BRIEF script has scarcely been altered. This makes me hope that I am not a radio writer, but simply a writer profoundly grateful to have discovered so varied and universal an audience, an audience which gives dramatic writers the scope of nineteenth-century novelists, allowing them a hearing only rivalled by that enjoyed by certain bullfighters, football players and "pop" singers in our century.

When THE DOCK BRIEF was to be presented in the theatre the problem arose of writing a play to go with it. The task was narrowed down by the fact that the new play had to provide contrasting parts for the two actors who played in THE DOCK BRIEF. Furthermore I was determined to write a second part that Michael Hordern would want to play, as I was naturally anxious he and no one else should appear as the seedy barrister in THE DOCK BRIEF, to my mind a miraculous performance in a part no other actor has yet attempted. Finally I had about eight weeks in which to produce the companion play. At first I found all these considerations as stimulating to thought as a loaded pistol pressed against the ear. In the end I achieved a sort of calm. I saw Michael Hordern as desperately gay, a faded Don Juan of the Earls Court Road.

9

I pictured his shiny blue blazer, his well-rubbed suède shoes. In a moment of abandon I gave him a ukulele and he has now, added to his other talents, a painfully acquired skill on this unlikely instrument. WHAT SHALL WE TELL CAROLINE? *got written and went into production. We had a double bill of plays to be performed on the same evening: to my surprise I found I had written a play which I believe is better than* THE DOCK BRIEF. *I think it more ambitious and more true. It has given rise to considerable argument among people connected with the theatre as to its precise meaning. In this argument I have been, I am afraid, of singularly little help.*

Two plays for the price of one is a proposition which is often not thought to be as attractive as it sounds. One set of characters digested, one situation explained and the audience is asked, exhausted by the struggle for small, warm, curiously unintoxicating, drinks at the bar, to grapple with new characters, strange situations. The mind, as often as not, boggles. If the first play is enjoyed, the audience may well reach for its coat and go home satisfied to dinner in the interval: if it is disliked there is no incentive to stay and discover if the story is really going to turn out as horribly as the first act threatens. The interval is clearly perilous: the transition difficult. In these two plays I had hoped the transition would not be too abrupt: in any event the locale was familiar, the first being set in a prison cell, the other in a boys' "preparatory" school in that fatally healthy seaside resort, Cold Sands on the Norfolk coast.

Other points of similarity might emerge. The plays are both intended as comedy, comedy being, to my mind, the only thing worth writing in this despairing age, provided the comedy is truly on the side of the lonely, the neglected, the unsuccessful, and plays its part in the war against established rules and against the imposing of an arbitrary code of behaviour upon individual and unpredictable human beings.

There may, for all I know, be great and funny plays to be written about successful lawyers, brilliant criminals, wise schoolmasters, or families where the children can grow up without silence and without regret. There are many plays that show that the law is always majestic or that family life is simple and easy to endure. Speaking for myself I am not on the side of such plays and a writer of comedy must choose his side with particular care. He cannot afford to aim at the defenceless, nor can he, like the more serious writer, treat any character with contempt.

In all plays, as in any sort of writing, what is important is the moment of recognition. The small time when you realise, sitting in a theatre, with a shock of excitement and unease, that you are watching yourself. In two plays it was perhaps too much to hope for a double recognition. But it might be that at some time in the course of the evening all parents and children would see their remoteness mirrored and the lawyers and criminals in the audience might even recognise their close affinity.

Up till now I SPY has not been performed on the stage. It has been done on the radio, and on television. Television, in England in the last few years, has gone through a startling and rapid period of evolution. To my mind it has, as a writer's medium, enormous advantages. Television has never been, and never can be smart. To the readers of Vogue *and the patrons of the Curzon cinema it remains the telly, the joke box, the thing our daily woman has, because of course she is so much richer than we. To millions of people it is a vital source of stimulation and entertainment. It is without a censor, and politically and socially controversial in a way the radio in England has never attempted to be.*

For a writer, television now seems to me the best medium after the theatre. The English have never shown much aptitude for making films, and in its present state our film industry, run as it almost entirely is, by chartered accountants, offers no outlet for creative talent. Sentimentalised patriotism, glossy nostalgia for a remote war, mirthless comedies about social situations which do not exist outside the pages of women's magazines, have been for many years the height of achievement for the British film. The accountants, handling thousands of pounds, can afford nothing better. A television programme is done on a far smaller budget. THE DOCK BRIEF cost in all about £800. It is done in a hurry before the producers or civil servants or chartered accountants have time to notice exactly what is going on. A writer, in these circumstances, can get away with murder. It is entirely his fault if this is, up till now, about all he has got away with.

Working in television I have never had it suggested that I should write at anything other than the best I can possibly do. I have never consciously written to please anyone but myself. I have never thought of the millions of nice people who, high officials in the television world have assured me, watch what I write. Had I done so I should scarcely have retained my sanity.

In England, where the cinema is moribund and there is no market for short stories, television should be embraced by writers with considerable enthusiasm. In fact very few important writers make use of this medium, and I cannot believe that they are so thoughtless as to be contemptuous of the television audience. Perhaps they are put off by the air of technical mystery with which people who know about television like to surround it. In fact there is nothing technical to be borne in mind when writing a television script. It is, it is true, difficult to end a scene on a girl in a bathing suit and start the next scene on the same girl in a different set in full evening dress; but even this is a difficulty which can be overcome if the story requires it. Some people write television scripts which are full of mysterious phrases such as "End telecine" or "Mix". These are quite unnecessary and their insertion only serves to irritate the producer.

The sadness of a television play is the shortness of its life, far shorter than those insects which are given, at least, twenty-four hours. As soon as a television play is over the stage hands move in to destroy the set. With the final fade-

12

out three weeks of rehearsal, miracles of technical planning and often performances of great beauty and intelligence vanish forever. For this reason television criticism is hampered, for it is useless to urge people to see a play the morning after it has been sent into oblivion. Television drama will grow up when every play is recorded, when the myth or mystery of live television is exploded and plays are at least repeated in a repertory system. If this stops the audience watching television every night and encourages us to live for an evening or so without entertainment it will do us and dramatic writing nothing but good.

As this is a book of plays I have re-written I SPY in a form which I believe will work on the stage, provided it is used by a producer of imagination who is not tied by the unities of time and place. Of these three plays I SPY surprised me most in its performance, it plays as a more embittered, savage little piece than reading it, or even writing it, had suggested. This is certainly no place to suggest how any of these plays should be presented; but any producer of I SPY should remember that the key scene is that between the lawyer and detective in the hotel dining room, a scene which contains words so wounding that the tender-hearted actor who played the lawyer was, at rehearsals, extremely reluctant to say them. Mrs. Morgan is, I think, the only really completely "good" character from a moral point of view I have ever enjoyed writing about. My pleasure in this character is now inseparable in my mind from the memory of Brenda Bruce who created her: in this play, as in WHAT SHALL WE TELL CAROLINE?, she gave a performance of great warmth and intelligence which never varied and was almost perfect from the first rehearsal. "When you've got Brenda Bruce's face on the screen," a television executive told me while watching I SPY, you don't need all those words you've written." I think he may well have been right. Every good piece of dramatic writing must contain passages where the words are inadequate to express the full emotion of the characters. A novelist is, of *necessity, slow to learn this; only a close study of very good acting can teach him.*

These three plays as I re-read them, represent for me weeks of placid enjoyment, weeks when I could perhaps have been more productively employed but during which I told myself I was being useful by standing in rehearsal rooms, draughty youth clubs, superannuated Baptist Chapels, with chalk marks at my feet and warm cups of meat-flavoured coffee in my hands. They represent wonderful dark Sunday afternoons in the stalls of theatres, empty but for roving pairs of enormous, mouse-swollen, theatrical cats. They also recall the agony of two opening nights; but on the whole the balance is on the side of pleasure, a pleasure due to the actors and actresses who played in them: and to whom this book is dedicated, with affection and respect.

Cromer Hall,
Norfolk.

April, 1958.

THE DOCK BRIEF

First produced by the B.B.C Third Programme on
May 12, 1957. The cast was as follows:

MORGENHALL   *Michael Hordern*
FOWLE   *David Kossoff*

Produced by Nesta Pain

On September 16, 1957 the play was produced on
B.B.C television with the same cast and producer.

Michael Codron with David Hall (for Talbot Productions Ltd.) presented the play in a double bill
(with *What Shall We Tell Caroline?*) at the Lyric
Opera House, Hammersmith, on April 9, 1958, and
on May 20, 1958 at the Garrick Theatre. The cast
was as follows:

MORGENHALL   *Michael Hordern*
FOWLE   *Maurice Denham*

Directed by Stuart Burge
Designed by Disley Jones

Scene One

A cell. The walls are grey and fade upwards into the shadows, so that the ceiling is not seen, and it might even be possible to escape upwards. The door is Right. Back stage is a high, barred window through which the sky looks very blue. Under the window is a stool. Against the Left wall is a bench with a wooden cupboard next to it. On the cupboard a wash basin, a towel and a Bible.

A small fat prisoner is standing on the stool on tip toes, his hands in his pockets. His eyes are on the sky.

Bolts shoot back. The door opens. Morgenhall strides in. He is dressed in a black gown and bands, an aged barrister with the appearance of a dusty vulture. He speaks off stage, to the warder.

MORGENHALL (*to an unseen warder*): Is this where. . . . you keep Mr. Fowle? Good, excellent. Then leave us alone like a kind fellow. Would you mind closing the door? These old places are so draughty.

[*The door closes. The bolts shoot back.*]

Mr. Fowle. . . . Where are you, Mr. Fowle? Not escaped, I pray. Good Heavens man, come down. Come down, Mr. Fowle.

[*He darts at him, and there is a struggle as he pulls down the bewildered Fowle.*]

I haven't hurt you?

[*Fowle : negative sounding noise.*]

I was suddenly anxious. A man in your unfortunate position. Desperate measures. And I couldn't bear to lose you. . . . No, don't stand up. It's difficult for you without braces, or a belt, I can see. And no tie, no shoe-laces. I'm so glad they're looking after you. You must forgive me if I frightened you just a little, Mr. Fowle. It was when I saw you up by that window. . . .

FOWLE (*a hoarse and sad voice*): Epping Forest.

MORGENHALL: What did you say?

FOWLE: I think you can see Epping Forest.

MORGENHALL: No doubt you can. But why, my dear chap, why should you want to?

FOWLE: It's the home stretch.

MORGENHALL: Very well.

FOWLE: I thought I could get a glimpse of the green. Between the chimneys and that shed. . . .

[*Fowle starts to climb up again. A brief renewed struggle.*]

MORGENHALL: No, get down. It's not wise to be up there, forever trying to look out. There's a draughty, sneeping wind. Treacherous.

FOWLE: Treacherous?

MORGENHALL: I'm afraid so. You never know what a mean, sneeping wind can do. Catch you by the throat, start a sneeze, then a dry tickle on the chest. I don't want anything to catch you like that before. . . .

FOWLE: Before what?

MORGENHALL: You're much better sitting quietly down there in the warm. Just sit quietly and I'll introduce myself.

FOWLE: I am tired.

MORGENHALL: I'm Wilfred Morgenhall.

FOWLE: Wilfred?

MORGENHALL: Morgenhall. The barrister.

FOWLE: The barrister?

MORGENHALL: Perfectly so. . . .

FOWLE: I'm sorry.

MORGENHALL: Why?

FOWLE: A barrister. That's very bad.

MORGENHALL: I don't know. Why's it so bad?

FOWLE: When a gentleman of your stamp goes wrong. A long fall.

MORGENHALL: What can you mean?

FOWLE: Different for an individual like me. I only kept a small seed shop.

MORGENHALL: Seed shop? My poor fellow. We mustn't let this unfortunate little case confuse us. We're going to remain very calm, very lucid. We're going to come to important decisions. Now, do me a favour, Mr. Fowle, no more seed shops.

FOWLE: Birdseed, of course. Individuals down our way kept birds mostly. Canaries and budgies. The budgies talked. Lot of lonely people down our way. They kept them for the talk.

MORGENHALL: Mr. Fowle. I'm a barrister.

FOWLE: Tragic.

MORGENHALL: I know the law.

FOWLE: It's trapped you.

MORGENHALL: I'm here to help you.

FOWLE: We'll help each other.

[*Pause.*]

MORGENHALL (*laughs uncontrollably*): I see. Mr. Fowle. I see where you've been bewildered. You think I'm in trouble as well. Then I've got good news for you at last. I'm free. Oh yes. I can leave here when I like.

FOWLE: You can?

MORGENHALL: The police are my friends.

FOWLE: They are?

MORGENHALL: And I've never felt better in my life. There now. That's relieved you, hasn't it? I'm not in any trouble.

FOWLE: Family all well?

MORGENHALL: I never married.

FOWLE: Rent paid up?

MORGENHALL: A week or two owing perhaps. Temporary lull in business. This case will end all that.

FOWLE: Which case?

MORGENHALL: Your case.

FOWLE: My....?

MORGENHALL: Case.

FOWLE: Oh that—it's not important.

MORGENHALL: Not?

FOWLE: I don't care about it to any large extent. Not as at present advised.

MORGENHALL: Mr. Fowle. How could you say that?

FOWLE: The flavour's gone out of it.

MORGENHALL: But we're only at the beginning.

FOWLE: I can't believe it's me concerned....

MORGENHALL: But it is you, Mr. Fowle. You mustn't let yourself forget that. You see, that's why you're here....

FOWLE: I can't seem to bother with it.

MORGENHALL: Can you be so busy?

FOWLE: Slopping in, slopping out. Peering at the old forest. It fills in the day.

MORGENHALL: You seem, if I may say so, to have adopted an unpleasantly selfish attitude.

FOWLE: Selfish?

MORGENHALL: Dog in the manger.

FOWLE: In the?

MORGENHALL: Unenthusiastic.

FOWLE: You're speaking quite frankly, I well appreciate....

MORGENHALL: I'm sorry, Fowle. You made me say it. There's so much of this about nowadays. There's so much ready made entertainment. Free billiards, National Health. Television. There's not the spirit abroad there used to be.

FOWLE: You feel that?

MORGENHALL: Whatever I've done I've always been mustard keen on my work. I've never lost the vision, Fowle. In all my disappointments I've never lost the love of the job.

FOWLE: The position in life you've obtained to.

MORGENHALL: Years of study I had to put in. It didn't just drop in my lap.

FOWLE: I've never studied. . . .

MORGENHALL: Year after year, Fowle, my window at college was alight until two a.m. There I sat among my books. I fed mainly on herrings. . . .

FOWLE: Lean years?

MORGENHALL: And black tea. No subsidised biscuits then, Fowle, no County Council tobacco, just work. . . .

FOWLE: Book work, almost entirely? I'm only assuming that, of course.

MORGENHALL: Want to hear some Latin?

FOWLE: Only if you have time.

MORGENHALL: Actus non sit reus nisi mens sit rea. Filius nullius. In flagrante delicto. Understand it?

FOWLE: I'm no scholar.

MORGENHALL: You most certainly are not. But I had to be, we all had to be in my day. Then we'd sit for the examinations, Mods, Smalls, Greats, Tripos, Little Goes, week after week, rowing men fainting, Indian students vomiting with fear, and no creeping out for a peep at the book under the pretext of a pump ship or getting a glance at the other fellow's celluloid cuff. . . .

FOWLE: That would be unheard of?

MORGENHALL: Then weeks, months of waiting. Nerve racking. Go up to the Lake District. Pace the mountains, play draughts, forget to huff. Then comes the fatal postcard.

FOWLE: What's it say?

MORGENHALL: Satisfied the examiners.

FOWLE: At last!

MORGENHALL: Don't rejoice so soon. True enough I felt I'd turned a corner, got a fur hood, bumped on the head with a Bible. Bachelor of Law sounded sweet in my ears. I thought of celebrating, a few kindred spirits round for a light ale. Told the only lady in my life that in five years' time perhaps....

FOWLE: You'd arrived.

MORGENHALL: That's what I thought when they painted my name up on my London chambers. I sat down to fill in the time until they sent my first brief in a real case. I sat down to do the crossword puzzle while I waited. Five years later, Fowle, what was I doing....

FOWLE: A little charge of High Treason?

MORGENHALL: I was still doing the crossword puzzle.

FOWLE: But better at it?

MORGENHALL: Not much. Not very much. As the years pass there come to be clues you no longer understand.

FOWLE: So all that training?

MORGENHALL: Wasted. The talents rust.

FOWLE: And the lady?

MORGENHALL: Drove an ambulance in the 1914. A stray piece of shrapnel took her. I don't care to talk of it.

FOWLE: Tragic.

MORGENHALL: What was?

FOWLE: Tragic my wife was never called up.

MORGENHALL: You mustn't talk like that, Fowle, your poor wife.

FOWLE: Don't let's carry on about me.

MORGENHALL: But we must carry on about you. That's what I'm here for.

FOWLE: You're here to?

MORGENHALL: Defend you.

FOWLE: Can't be done.

MORGENHALL: Why ever not?

FOWLE: I know who killed her.

MORGENHALL: Who?

FOWLE: Me.

[*Pause.*]

MORGENHALL (*considerable thought before he says*): Mr. Fowle, I have all the respect in the world for your opinions, but we must face this. You're a man of very little education. . . .

FOWLE: That's true.

MORGENHALL: One has only to glance at you. At those curious lobes to your ears. At the line of your hair. At the strange way your eyebrows connect in the middle, to see that you're a person of very limited intelligence.

FOWLE: Agreed, quite frankly.

MORGEHNALL: You think you killed your wife.

FOWLE: Seems so to me.

MORGENHALL: Mr. Fowle. Look at yourself objectively. On questions of birdseed I have no doubt you may be infallible—but on a vital point like this might you not be mistaken. . . . Don't answer. . . .

FOWLE: Why not, sir?

MORGENHALL: Before you drop the bomb of a reply, consider who will be wounded. Are the innocent to suffer?

FOWLE: I only want to be honest.

MORGENHALL: But you're a criminal, Mr. Fowle. You've broken through the narrow fabric of honesty. You are free to be kind, human, to do good.

FOWLE: But what I did to her. . . .

MORGENHALL: She's passed, you know, out of your life. You've set up new relationships. You've picked out me.

FOWLE: Picked out?

MORGENHALL: Selected.

FOWLE: But I didn't know. . . .

MORGENHALL: No, Mr. Fowle. That's the whole beauty of it. You didn't know me. You came to me under a system of chance invented, like the football pools, to even out the harsh inequality of a world where you have to deserve success. You, Mr. Fowle, are my first Dock Brief.

FOWLE: Your Dock?

MORGENHALL: Brief.

FOWLE: You couldn't explain?

MORGENHALL: Of course. Prisoners with no money and no friends exist. Luckily, you're one of them. They're entitled to choose any barrister sitting in Court to defend them. The barrister, however old, gets a brief, and is remunerated on a modest scale. Busy lawyers, wealthy lawyers, men with other interests, creep out of Court bent double when the Dock Brief is chosen. We regulars who are not busy sit on. I've been a regular for years. It's not etiquette, you see, even if you want the work, to wave at the prisoner, or whistle, or try to catch his eye by hoisting any sort of little flag.

FOWLE: Didn't know.

MORGENHALL: But you *can* choose the most advantageous seat. The seat any criminal would naturally point at. It's the seat under the window and for ten

26

years my old friend Tuppy Morgan, bagged it each day at ten. He sat there, reading Horace, and writing to his unnumerable aunts, and almost once a year a criminal pointed him out. Oh, Mr. Fowle, Tuppy was a limpet on that seat. But this morning, something, possibly a cold, perhaps death, kept him indoors. So I had his place. And you spotted me, no doubt.

FOWLE: Spotted you?

MORGENHALL: My glasses polished. My profile drawn and learned in front of the great window.

FOWLE: I never noticed.

MORGENHALL: But when they asked you to choose a lawyer?

FOWLE: I shut my eyes and pointed—I've picked horses that way, and football teams. Never did me any good, though, by any stretch of the imagination.

MORGENHALL: So even you, Mr. Fowle, didn't choose me?

FOWLE: Not altogether.

MORGENHALL: The law's a haphazard business.

FOWLE: It does seem chancy.

MORGENHALL: Years of training, and then to be picked out like a football pool.

FOWLE: Don't take it badly, sir.

MORGENHALL: Of course, you've been fortunate.

FOWLE: So unusual. I was never one to draw the free bird at Christmas, or guess the weight of the cake. Now I'm sorry I told you.

MORGENHALL: Never mind. You hurt me temporarily, Fowle, I must confess. It might have been kinder to have kept me in ignorance. But now it's done. Let's get down to business. And, Fowle—

FOWLE: Yes, sir.

MORGENHALL: Remember you're dealing with

fellow man. A man no longer young. Remember the hopes I've pinned on you and try. . . .

FOWLE: Try?

MORGENHALL: Try to spare me more pain.

FOWLE: I will, sir. Of course I will.

MORGENHALL: Now. Let's get our minds in order.

FOWLE: Sort things out.

MORGENHALL: Exactly. Now, this wife of yours.

FOWLE: Doris?

MORGENHALL: Doris. A bitter, unsympathetic woman?

FOWLE: She was always cheerful. She loved jokes.

MORGENHALL: Oh, Fowle. Do be very careful.

FOWLE: I will, sir. But if you'd known Doris. . . . She laughed harder than she worked. "Thank God," she'd say, "for my old English sense of fun."

MORGENHALL: What sort of jokes, Fowle, did this Doris appreciate?

FOWLE: All sorts. Pictures in the paper. Jokes on the wireless set. Laughs out of crackers, she'd keep them from Christmas to Christmas and trot them out in August.

MORGENHALL: You couldn't share it?

FOWLE: Not to that extent. I often missed the funny point.

MORGENHALL: Then you'd quarrel?

FOWLE: "Don't look so miserable, it may never happen." She said that every night when I came home. "Where'd you get that miserable expression from?"

MORGENHALL: I can see it now. There is a kind of Sunday evening appearance to you.

FOWLE: I was quite happy. But it was always "Cat got your tongue?" "Where's the funeral?" "Play us a tune on that old fiddle face of yours. Lucky there's one of us here that can see the funny side." Then we had to have our tea with the wireless on, so that she'd pick up the phrases.

MORGENHALL: You're not a wireless lover?

FOWLE: I couldn't always laugh. And she'd be doubled up across the table, gasping as if her lungs were full of water. "Laugh," she'd call, "Laugh, damn you. What've you got to be so miserable about?" Then she'd go under, bubbling like a drowning woman.

MORGENHALL: Made meals difficult?

FOWLE: Indigestible. I would have laughed, but the jokes never tickled me.

MORGENHALL: They tickled her?

FOWLE: Anything did. Anything a little comic. Our names were misfortunate.

MORGENHALL: Your names?

FOWLE: Fowle. Going down the aisle she said: "Now we're cock and hen, aren't we, old bird?" Coming away, it was "Now I'm Mrs. Fowle, you'll have to play fair with me." She laughed so hard we couldn't get her straightened up for the photograph.

MORGENHALL: Fond of puns, I gather you're trying to say.

FOWLE: Of any sort of joke. I had a little aviary at the bottom of my garden. As she got funnier so I spent more time with my birds. Budgerigars are small parrots. Circles round their eyes give them a sad, tired look.

MORGENHALL: You found them sympathetic?

FOWLE: Restful. Until one of them spoke out at me.

MORGENHALL: Spoke—what words?

FOWLE: "Don't look so miserable, it may never happen."

MORGENHALL: The bird said that?

FOWLE: She taught it during the day when I was out at work. It didn't mean to irritate.

MORGENHALL: It was wrong of her of course. To lead on your bird like that.

FOWLE: But it wasn't him that brought me to it. It was Bateson, the lodger.

MORGENHALL: Another man?

FOWLE: At long last.

MORGENHALL: I can see it now. A crime of passion. An unfaithful wife. *In flagrante.* . . . Of course, you don't know what that means. We'll reduce it to manslaughter right away. A wronged husband and there's never a dry eye in the jury-box. You came in and caught them.

FOWLE: Always laughing together.

MORGENHALL: Maddening.

FOWLE: He knew more jokes than she did.

MORGENHALL: Stealing her before your eyes?

FOWLE: That's what I thought. He was a big man. Ex-police. Said he'd been the scream of the station. I picked him for her specially. In the chitty I put up in the local sweet shop, I wrote: "Humorous type of lodger wanted."

MORGENHALL: But wasn't that a risk?

FOWLE: Slight, perhaps. But it went all right. Two days after he came he poised a bag of flour to fall on her in the kitchen. Then she sewed up the legs of his pyjamas. They had to hold on to each other so as not to fall over laughing. "Look at old misery standing there," she said. "He can never see anything subtle."

MORGENHALL: Galling for you. Terribly galling.

FOWLE: I thought all was well. I spent more time with the birds. I'd come home late and always be careful to scrunch the gravel at the front door. I went to bed early and left them with the Light Programme. On Sunday mornings I fed the budgies and suggested he took her tea in bed. "Laughter," "she read out from her horoscope, leads to love, even for those born under the sign of the Virgin."

MORGENHALL: You trusted them. They deceived you.

FOWLE: They deceived me all right. And I trusted them. Especially after I'd seen her on his knee and them both looking at the cartoons from one wrapping of chips.

MORGENHALL: Mr. Fowle. I'm not quite getting the drift of your evidence. My hope is—your thought may not prove a shade too involved for our literal-minded judge. Old Tommy Banter was a Rugger blue in '98. He never rose to chess and his draughts had a brutal, unintelligent quality.

FOWLE: When he'd first put his knee under her I thought he'd do the decent thing. I thought I'd have peace in my little house at last. The wireless set dead silent. The end of all that happy laughter. No sound but the twitter from the end of the garden and the squeak of my own foot on the linoleum.

MORGENHALL: You wanted. . . .

FOWLE: I heard them whispering together and my hopes raised high. Then I came back and he was gone.

MORGENHALL: She'd. . . .

FOWLE: Turned him out. Because he was getting over familiar. " I couldn't have that. " she said. " I may like my laugh, but thank God, I'm still respectable. No thank you, there's safety in marriage. So I'm stuck with you, fiddle face. Let's play a tune on it, shall we? " She'd sent him away, my last hope.

MORGENHALL: So you. . . .

FOWLE: I realise I did wrong.

MORGENHALL: You could have left.

FOWLE: Who'd have fed the birds? That thought was uppermost.

MORGENHALL: So it's not a crime of passion?

FOWLE: Not if you put it like that.

MORGENHALL: Mr. Fowle. I've worked and waited for you. Now, you're the only case I've got, *and* the most difficult.

FOWLE: I'm sorry.

MORGENHALL: A man could crack his head against a case like you and still be far from a solution. Can't you see how twelve honest hearts will snap like steel when they learn you ended up your wife because she *wouldn't* leave you?

FOWLE: If she had left, there wouldn't have been the need.

MORGENHALL: There's no doubt about it. As I look at you now, I see you're an unsympathetic figure.

FOWLE: There it is.

MORGENHALL: It'll need a brilliant stroke to save you. An unexpected move—something pulled out of a hat—I've got it. Something really exciting. The surprise witness.

FOWLE: Witness?

MORGENHALL: Picture the scene, Mr. Fowle. The Court room silent. The jury about to sink you. The prosecution flushed with victory. And then I rise, my voice a hoarse whisper, exhausted by that long trial. "My Lord. If your Lordship pleases."

FOWLE: What are you saying?

MORGENHALL: Do you expect me to do this off the cuff, Fowle, with no sort of rehearsal?

FOWLE: No. . . .

MORGENHALL: Take the stool and co-operate, man. Now, that towel over your head, please, to simulate the dirty grey wig—already you appear anonymous and vaguely alarming.

[*Morgenhall arranges Fowle on the stool. Drapes the towel over his head.*]

32

Now, my dear Fowle, forget your personality. You're Sir Tommy Banter, living with a widowed sister in a draughty great morgue on Wimbledon Common. Digestion, bad. Politics, an independent moral conservative. Favourite author, doesn't read. Diversions, snooker in the basement of the morgue, peeping at the lovers on the Common and money being given away on the television. In love with capital punishment, corporal punishment, and a younger brother who is accomplished at embroidery. A small, alarmed man, frightened of the great dog he lives with to give him the air of a country squire. Served with distinction in the Great War at sentencing soldiers to long terms of imprisonment. A man without friends, unexpectedly adored by a great-niece, three years old.

FOWLE: I am?

MORGENHALL: Him.

FOWLE: It feels strange.

MORGENHALL: Now, my Lord. I ask your Lordship's leave to call the surprise witness.

FOWLE: Certainly.

MORGENHALL: What?

FOWLE: Certainly.

MORGENHALL: For Heaven's sake, Fowle, this is like practising bull-fights with a kitten. Here's an irregular application by the defence, something that might twist the trial in the prisoner's favour and prevent you catching the connection at Charing Cross. Your breakfast's like a leadweight on your chest, your sister, plunging at Spot last night, ripped the cloth. The dog bit your ankle on the way downstairs. No, blind yourself with rage and terrible justice.

FOWLE: No. You can't call the surprise witness.

33

MORGENHALL: That's better. Oh, my Lord. If your Lordship would listen to me.

FOWLE: Certainly not. You've had your chance. Let's get on with it.

MORGENHALL: My Lord. Justice must not only be done, but must clearly be seen to be done. No one knows, as yet, what my surprise witness will say. Perhaps he'll say the prisoner is guilty in his black heart as your Lordship thinks. But perhaps, gentlemen of the jury, we have trapped an innocent. If so, shall we deny him the one door through which he might walk to freedom? The public outcry would never die down.

FOWLE (*snatching off the towel and rising angrily to his feet*): Hear, hear!

MORGENHALL: What's that?

FOWLE: The public outcry.

MORGENHALL: Excellent. Now, towel back on. You're the judge.

FOWLE (*as the Judge*): Silence! I'll have all those noisy people put out. Very well. Call the witness. But keep it short.

MORGENHALL: Wonderful. Very good. Now. Deathly silence as the witness walks through the breathless crowds. Let's see the surprise witness. Take the towel off.

FOWLE (*moves from the stool and, standing very straight says*): I swear to tell the truth. . . .

MORGENHALL: You've got a real feeling for the Law. A pity you came to it so late in life.

FOWLE: The whole truth.

MORGENHALL: Now, what's your name?

FOWLE (*absent minded*): Herbert Fowle.

MORGENHALL: No, no. You're the witness.

FOWLE: Martin Jones.

MORGENHALL: Excellent. Now, you know Herbert

Fowle?

FOWLE: All my life.

MORGENHALL: Always found him respectable?

FOWLE: Very quiet spoken man, and clean living.

MORGENHALL: Where was he when this crime took place?

FOWLE: He was. . . .

MORGENHALL: Just a moment. My Lord, will you sharpen a pencil and note this down?

FOWLE: You'd dare to say that? To him?

MORGENHALL: Fearlessness, Mr. Fowle. The first essential in an advocate. Is your Lordship's pencil poised?

FOWLE (*as Judge*): Yes, yes. Get on with it.

MORGENHALL: Where was he?

FOWLE (*as Witness*): In my house.

MORGENHALL: All the evening?

FOWLE: Playing whist. I went to collect him and we left Mrs. Fowle well and happy. I returned with him and she'd been removed to the Country and General.

MORGENHALL: Panic stirs the prosecution benches. The prosecutor tries a few fumbling questions. But you stand your ground, don't you?

FOWLE: Certainly.

MORGENHALL: My Lord. I demand the prisoner be released.

FOWLE (*as Judge*): Certainly. Can't think what all this fuss has been about. Release the prisoner, and reduce all police officers in Court to the rank of P.C.

[*Pause.*]

MORGENHALL: Fowle.

FOWLE: Yes, sir.

MORGENHALL: Aren't you going to thank me?

FOWLE: I don't know what I can say.

MORGENHALL: Words don't come easily to you, do they?

FOWLE: Very hard.

MORGENHALL: You could just stand and stammer in a touching way and offer me that old gold watch of your father's.

FOWLE: But. . . .

MORGENHALL: Well, I think we've pulled your chestnut out of the fire. We'll just have to make sure of this fellow Jones.

FOWLE: But. . . .

MORGENHALL: Fowle, you're a good simple chap, but there's no need to interrupt my thinking.

FOWLE: I was only reminding you. . . .

MORGENHALL: Well, what?

FOWLE: We have no Jones.

MORGENHALL: Carried off in a cold spell? Then we can get his statement in under the Evidence Act.

FOWLE: He never lived. We made him up.

[*Pause.*]

MORGENHALL: Fowle.

FOWLE: Yes, sir.

MORGENHALL: It's a remarkable thing, but with no legal training, I think you've put your finger on a fatal weakness in our defence.

FOWLE: I was afraid it might be so.

MORGENHALL: It is so.

FOWLE: Then we'd better just give in.

MORGENHALL: Give in? We do not give in. When my life depends on this case.

FOWLE: I forgot. Then, we must try.

MORGENHALL: Yes. Brain! Brain! Go to work. It'll come to me, you know, in an illuminating flash.

Hard, relentless brain work. This is the way I go at the crosswords and I never give up. I have it. Bateson!

FOWLE: The lodger?

MORGENHALL: Bateson, the lodger. I never liked him. Under a ruthless cross-examination, you know, he might confess that it was he. Do you see a flash?

FOWLE: You look much happier.

MORGENHALL: I am much happier. And when I begin my ruthless cross-examination. . . .

FOWLE: Would you care to try it?

MORGENHALL: Mr. Fowle. You and I are learning to muck in splendidly together over this. Mr. Bateson.

FOWLE (*as Bateson, lounging in an imaginary witness box with his hands in his pockets*): Yes. Sir?

MORGENHALL: Perhaps, when you address the Court you'd be good enough to take your hands out of your pockets. Not you Mr. Fowle, of course. You became on very friendly terms with the prisoner's wife?

FOWLE: We had one or two good old laughs together.

MORGENHALL: Was the association entirely innocent?

FOWLE: Innocent laughs. Jokes without offence. The cracker or Christmas card variety. No jokes that would have shamed a postcard.

MORGENHALL: And to tell those innocent jokes, did you have to sit very close to Mrs. Fowle?

FOWLE: How do you mean?

MORGENHALL: Did you have to sit beneath her?

FOWLE: I don't understand.

MORGENHALL: Did she perch upon your knee?

FOWLE (*horrified intake of breath*).

MORGENHALL: What was that?

FOWLE: Shocked breathing from the jury, sir.

MORGENHALL: Having its effect, eh? Now, Mr. Bateson. Will you kindly answer my question.

FOWLE: You're trying to trap me.

MORGENHALL: Not trying, Bateson, succeeding.

FOWLE: Well, she may have rested on my knee. Once or twice.

MORGENHALL: And you loved her, guiltily?

FOWLE: I may have done.

MORGENHALL: And planned to take her away with you?

FOWLE: I did ask her.

MORGENHALL: And when she refused....

FOWLE (*as Judge*): Just a moment. Where's all this leading?

MORGENHALL: Your Lordship asks me! My Lord, it is our case that it was this man, Bateson, enraged by the refusal of the prisoner's wife to follow him, who struck.... You see where we've got to?

FOWLE: I do.

MORGENHALL: Masterly. I think you'll have to agree with me?

FOWLE: Of course.

MORGENHALL: No flaws in this one?

FOWLE: Not really a flaw, sir. Perhaps a little hitch.

MORGENHALL: A hitch. Go on. Break it down.

FOWLE: No, sir, really. Not after you've been so kind.

MORGENHALL: Never mind. All my life I've stood against the winds of criticism and neglect. My gown may be a little tattered, my cuffs frayed. There may be a hole in my sock for the draughts to get at me. Quite often, on my way to Court, I notice that my left shoe lets in water. I am used to hardship. Speak on, Mr. Fowle.

FOWLE: Soon as he left my house, Bateson was stopped by an officer. He'd lifted an alarm clock off

38

me, and the remains of a bottle of port. They booked him straight away.

MORGENHALL: You mean, there wasn't time?

FOWLE: Hardly. Two hours later the next door observed Mrs. Fowle at the washing. Then I came home.

MORGENHALL: Fowle. Do you want to help me?

FOWLE: Of course. Haven't I shown it?

MORGENHALL: But you will go on putting all these difficulties in my way.

FOWLE: I knew you'd be upset.

MORGENHALL: Not really. After all, I'm a grown up, even an old man. At my age one expects little gratitude. There's a cat I feed each day at my lodgings, a waitress in the lunch room here who always gets that sixpence under my plate. In ten, twenty years' time, will they remember me? Oh, I'm not bitter. But a little help, just a very little encouragement. . . .

FOWLE: But you'll win this case. A brilliant mind like yours.

MORGENHALL: Yes. Thank God. It's very brilliant.

FOWLE: And all that training.

MORGENHALL: Years of it. Hard, hard training.

FOWLE: You'll solve it, sir.

[*Pause.*]

MORGENHALL: Fowle. Do you know what I've heard Tuppy Morgan say? After all, he's sat here, year in, year out, as long as anyone can remember, in Court, waiting for the Dock Brief himself. Wilfred, he's frequently told me, if they ever give you a brief, old fellow, attack the medical evidence. Remember, the jury's full of rheumatism and arthritis and shocking gastric troubles. They love to see a medical man put through it. Always go for a doctor.

FOWLE (*eagerly*): You'd like to try?

MORGENHALL: Shall we?

FOWLE: I'd enjoy it.

MORGENHALL: Doctor. Did you say the lady died of heart failure?

FOWLE (*as Doctor*): No.

MORGENHALL: Come, Doctor. Don't fence with me. Her heart wasn't normal when you examined her, was it?

FOWLE: She was dead.

MORGENHALL: So it had stopped.

FOWLE: Yes.

MORGENHALL: Then her heart had failed?

FOWLE: Well....

MORGENHALL: So she died of heart failure?

FOWLE: But....

MORGENHALL: And heart failure might have been brought on by a fit, I say a fit of laughter, at a curiously rich joke on the wireless?

FOWLE: Whew.

[*Fowle claps softly. Pause.*]

MORGENHALL: Thank you, Fowle. It was kind but, I thought, hollow. I don't believe my attack on the doctor was convincing.

FOWLE: Perhaps a bit unlikely. But clever....

MORGENHALL: Too clever. No. We're not going to win this on science, Fowle. Science must be thrown away. As I asked those questions, I saw I wasn't even convincing you of your own innocence. But you respond to emotion, Fowle, as I do, the magic of oratory, the wonderful power of words.

FOWLE: Now you're talking.

MORGENHALL: I'm going to talk.

FOWLE: I wish I could hear some of it. Words as grand as print.

MORGENHALL: A golden tongue. A voice like a lyre to charm you out of hell.

FOWLE: Now you've commenced to wander away from all I've understood.

MORGENHALL: I was drawing on the riches of my classical education which comforts me on buses, waiting at surgeries, or in prison cells. But I shall speak to the jury simply, without classical allusions. I shall say....

FOWLE: Yes.

MORGENHALL: I shall say....

FOWLE: What?

MORGENHALL: I had it on the tip of my tongue.

FOWLE: Oh.

MORGENHALL: I shan't disappoint you. I shall speak for a day, perhaps two days. At the end I shall say....

FOWLE: Yes. Just the closing words.

MORGENHALL: The closing words.

FOWLE: To clinch the argument.

MORGENHALL: Yes. The final, irrefutable argument.

FOWLE: If I could only hear.

MORGENHALL: You shall, Fowle. You shall hear it. In Court. It'll come out in Court, and when I sink back in my seat, trembling, and wipe the real tears off my glasses....

FOWLE: The judge's summing up.

MORGENHALL: What will Tommy say?

FOWLE (as Judge): Members of the jury....

MORGENHALL: Struggling with emotion as well.

FOWLE: I can't add anything to the words of the barrister. Go out and consider your verdict.

MORGENHALL: Have they left the box?

FOWLE: Only a formality.

MORGENHALL: I see. I wonder how long they'll be out. (*Pause.*) They're out a long time.

FOWLE: Of course, it must seem long to you. The suspense.

MORGENHALL: I hope they won't disagree.

FOWLE: I don't see how they can.

[*Pause.*]

MORGENHALL: Fowle.

FOWLE: Yes, sir.

MORGENHALL: Shall we just take a peep into the jury room.

FOWLE: I wish we could.

MORGENHALL: Let's. Let me see, you're the foreman?

FOWLE: I take it we're all agreed, chaps. So let's sit here and have a short smoke.

[*They sit on the bench together.*]

MORGENHALL: An excellent idea. The barrister saved him.

FOWLE: That wonderful speech. I had a bit of doubt before I heard the speech.

MORGENHALL: No doubt now, have you?

FOWLE: Certainly not.

[*They light imaginary pipes.*]

Care for a fill of mine?

MORGENHALL: Thank you so much. Match?

FOWLE: Here you are.

MORGENHALL: I say, you don't think the poor fellow's in any doubt, do you?

FOWLE: No. He must know he'll get off. After the speech I mean.

MORGENHALL: I mean, I wouldn't like him to be on pins. . . .

FOWLE: Think we ought to go back and reassure him?

[*They move off the bench.*]

MORGENHALL: As you wish. Careful that pipe doesn't start a fire in your pocket. (*As Clerk of Court*): Gentlemen of the jury. Have you considered your verdict?

FOWLE: We have.

MORGENHALL: And do you find the prisoner guilty or not guilty?

FOWLE: Not guilty, my Lord.

MORGENHALL: Hooray!

FOWLE (*as Judge*): Now, if there's any sort of Mafeking around, I'll have the Court closed.

MORGENHALL: So I'm surrounded, mobbed. Tuppy Morgan wrings my hand and says it was lucky he left the seat. The judge sends me a letter of congratulation. The journalists dart off to their little telephones. And what now: "Of course they'd make you a judge but you're probably too busy. . . ." There's a queue of solicitors on the stairs. . . . My old clerk writes on my next brief, a thousand guineas to divorce a duchess. There are questions of new clothes, laying down the port. Oh, Mr. Fowle, the change in life you've brought me.

FOWLE: It will be your greatest day.

MORGENHALL: Yes, Mr. Fowle. My greatest day.

[*The bolts shoot back, the door opens slowly.*]

What's that? I said we weren't to be interrupted.
It's draughty in here with that door open. Close it,
there's a good chap, do.

FOWLE: I think, you know, they must want us for
the trial.

[*Fowle goes through the door. Morgenhall follows with a
dramatic sweep of his gown.*]

The Curtain Falls.

Scene Two

*When the curtain rises again the sky through the windows
shows that it is late afternoon. The door is unlocked and
Morgenhall enters. He is without his wig and gown, more
agitated than ever, he speaks to the Warder, off stage.*

MORGENHALL: He's not here at the moment—he's
not. . . .? Oh, I'm so glad. Just out temporarily?
With the governor? Then, I'll wait for him. Poor
soul. How's he taking it? You're not allowed to
answer questions? The regulations, I suppose. Well,
you must obey the regulations. I'll just sit down here
and wait for Mr. Fowle.

[*The door closes.*]

(*He whistles. Whistling stops.*) May it please you, my
Lord, *members* of the jury. I should have said, may it
please you, my *Lord*, members of the jury. I should
have said. . . .

[*He begins to walk up and down.*]

Members of the jury. Is there one of you who doesn't
crave for peace . . . crave for peace. The silence of
an undisturbed life, the dignity of an existence
without dependents . . . without jokes. Have you
never been tempted?
I should have said. . . .
Members of the *jury*. You and I are men of the
world. If your Lordship would kindly not interrupt
my speech to the jury. I'm obliged. Members of the
jury, before I was so rudely interrupted.
I might have said. . . .
Look at the prisoner, members of the jury. Has he
hurt you, done you the slightest harm? Is he not the

45

mildest of men? He merely took it upon himself to regulate his domestic affairs. An Englishman's home is his castle. Do any of you feel a primitive urge, members of the jury, to be revenged on this gentle bird fancier. . . .

Members of the jury, I see I'm affecting your emotions but let us consider the weight of the evidence. . . I might have said that!

I might have said. . . . (*with distress*) I might have said something. . . .

[*The door opens. Fowle enters. He is smiling to himself, but as soon as he sees Morgenhall he looks serious and solicitous.*]

FOWLE: I was hoping you'd find time to drop in, sir. I'm afraid you're upset.

MORGENHALL: No, no, my dear chap. Not at all upset.

FOWLE: The result of the trial's upset you.

MORGENHALL: I feel a little dashed. A little out of sorts.

FOWLE: It was disappointing for you.

MORGENHALL: A touch of disappointment. But there'll be other cases. There may be other cases.

FOWLE: But you'd built such high hopes on this particular one.

MORGENHALL: Well, there it is, Fowle.

FOWLE: It doesn't do to expect too much of a particular thing.

MORGENHALL: You're right, of course.

FOWLE: Year after year I used to look forward keenly to the feathered friends fanciers' annual do. Invariably it took the form of a dinner.

MORGENHALL: Your yearly treat?

FOWLE: Exactly. All I had in the enjoyment line.

Each year I built high hopes on it. June 13th, I'd say,
now there's an evening to look forward to.

MORGENHALL: Something to live for?

FOWLE: In a way. But when it came, you know, it
was never up to it. Your collar was always too tight,
or the food was inadequate, or someone had a nasty
scene with the fancier in the chair. So, on June 14th, I
always said to myself: Thank God for a night at
home.

MORGENHALL: It came and went and your life didn't
change?

FOWLE: No, quite frankly.

MORGENHALL: And this case has left me just as I was
before.

FOWLE: Don't say that.

MORGENHALL: Tuppy Morgan's back in his old
seat under the window. The judge never congratu-
lated me. No one's rung up to offer me a brief. I
thought my old clerk looked coldly at me, and there
was a titter in the luncheon room when I ordered my
usual roll and tomato soup.

FOWLE: But I. . . .

MORGENHALL: And you're not left in a very favour-
able position.

FOWLE: Don't say that, sir. It's not so bad for me.
After all, I had no education.

MORGENHALL: So many years before I could master
the Roman Law relating to the ownership of
chariots. . . .

FOWLE: Wasted, you think?

MORGENHALL: I feel so.

FOWLE: But without that rich background, would
an individual have been able to sway the Court as
you did?

MORGENHALL: Sway?

FOWLE: The Court.

MORGENHALL: Did I do that?

FOWLE: It struck me you did.

MORGENHALL: Indeed. . . .

FOWLE: It's turned out masterly.

MORGENHALL: Mr. Fowle, you're trying to be kind. When I was a child I played French cricket with an uncle who deliberately allowed the ball to strike his legs. At the age of seven that irked me. At sixty-three I can face the difficulties of accurate batting. . . .

FOWLE: But no, sir. I really mean it. I owe it all to you. Where I am.

MORGENHALL: I'm afraid near the end.

FOWLE: Just commencing.

MORGENHALL: I lost, Mr. Fowle. You may not be aware of it. It may not have been hammered home to you yet. But your case is lost.

FOWLE: But there are ways and ways of losing.

MORGENHALL: That's true, of course.

FOWLE: I noticed your artfulness right at the start, when the policeman gave evidence. You pulled out that red handkerchief, slowly and deliberately, like a conjuring trick.

MORGENHALL: And blew?

FOWLE: A sad, terrible trumpet.

MORGENHALL: Unnerved him, I thought.

FOWLE: He never recovered. There was no call to ask questions after that.

MORGENHALL: And then they called that doctor.

FOWLE: You were right not to bother with him.

MORGENHALL: Tactics, you see. We'd decided not to trouble with science.

FOWLE: So we had. And with Bateson. . . .

MORGENHALL: No, Fowle. I must beware of your flattery, I think I might have asked Bateson. . . .

FOWLE: It wouldn't have made a farthing's difference. A glance told them he was a demon.

48

MORGENHALL: He stood there, so big and red, with his no tie and dirty collar. I rose up to question him and suddenly it seemed as if there were no reason for us to converse. I remembered what you said about his jokes, his familiarity with your wife. What had he and I in common? I turned from him in disgust. I think that jury guessed the reason for my silence with friend Bateson.

FOWLE: I think they did!

MORGENHALL: But when it came to the speech. . . .

FOWLE: The best stroke of all.

MORGENHALL: I can't agree. You no longer carry me with you.

FOWLE: Said from the heart.

MORGENHALL: I'm sure of it. But not, dare I say, altogether justified? We can't pretend, can we, Mr. Fowle, that the speech was a success?

FOWLE: It won the day.

MORGENHALL: I beg you not to be under any illusions. They found you guilty.

FOWLE: I was forgetting. But that masterly speech. . .

MORGENHALL: I can't be hoodwinked.

FOWLE: But you don't know. . . .

MORGENHALL: I stood up, Mr. Fowle, and it was the moment I'd waited for. Ambition had driven me to it, the moment when I was alone with what I wanted. Everyone turned to me, twelve blank faces in the jury box, eager to have the grumpy looks wiped off them. The judge was silent. The prosecutor court-eously pretended to be asleep. I only had to open my mouth and pour words out. What stopped me?

FOWLE: What?

MORGENHALL: Fear. That's what's suggested. That's what the clerks tittered to the waitresses in Friday's luncheon room. Old Wilf Morgenhall was in a funk.

FOWLE: More shame on them. . . .

MORGENHALL: But it wasn't so. Nor did my mind go blank. When I rose I knew exactly what I was going to say.

FOWLE: Then, why?

MORGENHALL: Not say it—you were going to say?

FOWLE: It had struck me—

MORGENHALL: It must have, Fowle. It must have struck many people. You'll forgive a reminiscence. . . .

FOWLE: Glad of one.

MORGENHALL: The lady I happened to mention yesterday. I don't of course, often speak of her. . . .

FOWLE: She, who, in the 1914. . . . ?

MORGENHALL: Exactly. But I lost her long before that. For years, you know, Mr. Fowle, this particular lady and I met at tea parties, tennis, and so on. Then, one evening, I walked home with her. We stood on Vauxhall Bridge, a warm Summer night, and silence fell. It was the moment when I should have spoken, the obvious moment. Then, something overcome me, it wasn't shyness or fear then, but a tremendous exhaustion. I was tired out by the long wait, and when the opportunity came—all I could think of was sleep.

FOWLE: It's a relief. . . .

MORGENHALL: To go home alone. To undress, clean your teeth, knock out your pipe, not to bother with failure or success.

FOWLE: So yesterday. . . .

MORGENHALL: I had lived through that moment so many times. It happened every day in my mind, daydreaming on buses, or in the doctor's surgery. When it came, I was tired of it. The exhaustion came over me. I wanted it to be all over. I wanted to be alone in my room, in the darkness, with a soft pillow round my ears. . . . So I failed.

FOWLE: Don't say it.

MORGENHALL: Being too tired to make my daydream public. It's a nice day. Summer's coming.

FOWLE: No, don't sir. Not too near the window.

MORGENHALL: Why not, Mr. Fowle?

FOWLE: I was concerned. A man in your position might be desperate. . . .

MORGENHALL: You say you can see the forest?

FOWLE: Just a splash of it.

MORGENHALL: I think I shall retire from the bar.

FOWLE: Don't say it, sir. After that rigorous training.

MORGENHALL: Well, there it is. I think I shall retire.

FOWLE: But cheer up, sir. As you said, other cases, other days. Let's take this calmly, sir. Let's be very lucid, as you put it in your own statement.

MORGENHALL: Other cases? I'm getting on, you know. Tuppy Morgan's back in his place. I doubt if the Dock Brief will come round again.

FOWLE: But there'll be something.

MORGENHALL: What can there be? Unless?

FOWLE: Yes, sir?

MORGENHALL: There would be another brief if. . . .

FOWLE: Yes?

MORGENHALL: I advised you to appeal. . . .

FOWLE: Ah, now that, misfortunately. . . .

MORGENHALL: There's a different atmosphere there, up in the Appeal Court, Fowle. It's far from the rough and tumble, question and answer, swear on the Bible and lie your way out of it. It's quiet up there, pure Law, of course. Yes. I believe I'm cut out for the Court of Appeal. . . .

FOWLE: But you see. . . .

MORGENHALL: A big, quiet Court in the early Summer afternoon. Piles of books, and when you put one down the dust and powdered leather rises

and makes the ushers sneeze. The clock ticks.
Three old judges in scarlet take snuff with trembling
hands. You'll sit in the dock and not follow a legal
word. And I'll give them all my Law and get you
off on a technicality.

FOWLE: But today. . . .

MORGENHALL: Now, if I may remind your Lordships
of Prickle against the Haverfordwest Justices *ex
parte* Anger, reported in 96 Moor's Ecclesiastical
at page a thousand and three. Have your Lordships
the report? Lord Bradwell, C. J., says, at the foot
of the page. " The guilty intention is a deep founda-
tion stone in the wall of our jurisprudence. So if it
be that Prickle did run the bailiff through with his
poignard taking him for a stray dog or cat, it seems
there would be well raised the plea of autrefois
mistake. But, contra, if he thought him to be his
neighbour's cat, then, as my Brother Breadwinkle
has well said in Lord Roche and Anderson, there
might fall out a constructive larceny and felo in
rem." Oh, Mr. Fowle, I have some of these fine
cases by heart.

FOWLE: Above me, I'm afraid, you're going now.

MORGENHALL: Of course I am. These cases always
bore the prisoner until they're upheld or overruled
and he comes out dead or alive at the end of it all.

FOWLE: I'd like to hear you reading them, though. . . .

MORGENHALL: You would. I'll be followed to
Court by my clerk, an old tortoise burdened by the
weight of authorities. Then he'll lay them out in a
fine buff and half calf row, a letter from a clergyman
I correspond with in Wales torn to mark each place.
A glass of water, a dry cough and the " My respectful
submission."

FOWLE: And that, of course, is. . . .

MORGENHALL: That the judge misdirected himself.

He forgot the rule in Rimmer's case, he confused his *mens sana*, he displaced the burden of proof, he played fast and loose with all reasonable doubt, he kicked the presumption of innocence round like a football.

FOWLE: Strong words.

MORGENHALL: I shan't let Tommy Banter off lightly.

FOWLE: The judge?

MORGENHALL: Thoroughly unscholarly. Not a word of Latin in the whole summing up.

FOWLE: Not up to you, of course.

MORGENHALL: Thank God, I kept my books. There have been times, Fowle, when I was tempted, pricked and harried for rent perhaps, to have my clerk barter the whole lot away for the few pounds they offer for centuries of entombed law. But I stuck to them. I still have my Swabey and Tristram, my Pod's *Privy Council*, my Spinks *Prize Cases*. I shall open them up and say . . . I shall say. . . .

FOWLE: It's no good.

MORGENHALL: What's no good?

FOWLE: It's no good appealing.

MORGENHALL: No good?

FOWLE: No good at all.

MORGENHALL: Mr. Fowle. I've worked hard for you.

FOWLE: True enough.

MORGENHALL: And I mean to go on working.

FOWLE: It's a great comfort. . . .

MORGENHALL: In the course of our close, and may I say it? yes, our happy collaboration on this little crime of yours, I've become almost fond of you.

FOWLE: Thank you, sir.

MORGENHALL: At first, I have to admit it, I was put off by your somewhat furtive and repulsive appearance. It's happened before. I saw, I quite agree, only the outer husk, and what I saw was a small man marked by all the physical signs of confirmed criminality.

FOWLE: No oil painting?

MORGENHALL: Let's agree on that at once.

FOWLE: The wife thought so, too.

MORGENHALL: Enough of her, poor woman.

FOWLE: Oh, agreed.

MORGENHALL: My first solicitude for your well-being, let's face up to this as well, had a selfish element. You were my very own case, and I didn't want to lose you.

FOWLE: Natural feelings. But still. . . .

MORGENHALL: I haven't wounded you?

FOWLE: Nothing fatal.

MORGENHALL: I'm glad. Because, you know, as we worked on this case together, an affection sprang up....

FOWLE: Mutual.

MORGENHALL: You seemed to have a real desire to help, and, if I may say so, an instinctive taste for the law.

FOWLE: A man can't go through this sort of thing without getting legal interests.

MORGENHALL: Quite so. And of course, as a self-made man, that's to your credit. But I did notice, just at the start, some flaws in you as a client.

FOWLE: Flaws?

MORGENHALL: You may not care to admit it. But let's be honest. After all, we don't want to look on the dreary side; but you may not be with us for very long. . . .

FOWLE: That's what I was trying to say. . . .

MORGENHALL: Please, Mr. Fowle, no interruptions until we've cleared this out of the way. Now didn't you, just at the beginning, put unnecesary difficulties before us?

FOWLE: Did I?

MORGENHALL: I well remember, before I got a bit of keenness into you, that you seemed about to admit your guilt.

FOWLE: Oh. . . .

MORGENHALL: Just a little obstinate, wasn't it?

FOWLE: I dare say. . . .

MORGENHALL: And now, when I've worked for fifty years to get the Law at my finger-tips, I hear you mutter, " No appeal."

FOWLE: No appeal!

MORGENHALL: Mr. Fowle. . . .

FOWLE: Yesterday you asked me to spare you pain, sir. This is going to be very hard for me.

MORGENHALL: What?

FOWLE: As you say, we've worked together, and I've had the pleasure of watching the ticking over of a legal mind. If you'd call any afternoon I'd be pleased to repay the compliment by showing you my birds. . . .

MORGENHALL: Not in this world you must realise, unless we appeal.

FOWLE: You see, this morning I saw the Governor.

MORGENHALL: You had some complaint?

FOWLE: I don't want to boast, but the truth is . . . he sent for me.

MORGENHALL: You went in fear. . . .

FOWLE: And trembling. But he turned out a very gentlemanly sort of individual. Ex-Army, I should imagine. All the ornaments of a gentleman. Wife and children in a tinted photo framed on the desk, handsome oil painting of a prize pig over the mantel-piece. Healthy red face. Strong smell of scented soap. . . .

MORGENHALL: But grow to the point. . . .

FOWLE: I'm telling you. " Well, Fowle " he says,

" Sit down do. I'm just finishing this letter." So I sat and looked out of his windows. Big wide windows in the Governor's office, and the view. . . .

MORGENHALL: Fowle. If this anecdote has any point, be a good little chap, reach it.

FOWLE: Of course it has, where was I?

MORGENHALL: Admiring the view as usual.

FOWLE: Panoramic it was. Well, this Governor individual, finishing his letter, lit up one of those flat type of Egyptian cigarettes. " Well, Fowle," he said. . . .

MORGENHALL: Yes, yes. It's not necessary, Fowle, to reproduce every word of this conversation. Give us the gist, just the meat, you understand. Leave out the trimmings.

FOWLE: Trimmings there weren't. He put it quite bluntly.

MORGENHALL: What did he put?

FOWLE: " Well, Fowle, this may surprise you. But the Home Office was on the telephone about you this morning." Isn't that a Government department?

MORGENHALL: Yes, yes, and well. . . .

FOWLE: It seems they do, in his words, come through from time to time, and just on business, of course, on that blower. And quite frankly, he admitted he was as shocked as I was. But the drill is, as he phrased it, a reprieve.

MORGENHALL: A . . .?

FOWLE: It's all over. I'm free. It seems that trial was no good at all. . . .

MORGENHALL: No good. But why?

FOWLE: Oh, no particular reason.

MORGENHALL: There must be a reason. Nothing passes in the Law without a reason.

FOWLE: You won't care to know.

MORGENHALL: Tell me.

FOWLE: You're too busy to wait. . . .

MORGENHALL: Tell me, Mr. Fowle. I beg of you. Tell me directly why this Governor, who knows nothing of the Law, should have called our one and only trial together " No good."

FOWLE: You yourself taught me not to scatter information like bombs.

MORGENHALL: Mr. Fowle. You must answer my question. My legal career may depend on it. If I'm not to have wasted my life on useless trials.

FOWLE: You want to hear?

MORGENHALL: Certainly.

FOWLE: He may not have been serious. There was a twinkle, most likely, in his eye.

MORGENHALL: But he said . . .

FOWLE: That the barrister they chose for me was no good. An old crock, in his words. No good at all. That he never said a word in my defence. So my case never got to the jury. He said the whole business was ever so null and void, but I'd better be careful in the future. . . .

[*Morgenhall runs across the cell, mounts the stool, begins to undo his tie.*]

No! Mr. Morgenhall! Come down from there! No, sir! Don't do it.

[*They struggle. Fowle brings Morgenhall to earth.*]

Don't you see? If I'd had a barrister who asked questions and made clever speeches I'd be as dead as mutton. Your artfulness saved me. . . .

MORGENHALL: My. . . .

FOWLE: The artful way you handled it. The dumb tactics. They paid off! I'm alive!

MORGENHALL: There is that. . . .

FOWLE: And so are you.

MORGENHALL: We both are?

FOWLE: I'm free.

MORGENHALL: To go back to your birds. I suppose. . . .

FOWLE: Yes, Mr. Morgenhall?

MORGENHALL: It's unlikely you'll marry again.

FOWLE: Unlikely.

[*Long pause.*]

MORGENHALL: But you have the clear appearance of a criminal. I suppose it's not impossible that you might commit some rather more trivial offence.

FOWLE: A man can't live, Mr. Morgenhall, without committing some trivial offences. Almost daily.

MORGENHALL: Then we may meet again. You may need my services. . . .

FOWLE: Constantly.

MORGENHALL The future may not be so black. . . .

FOWLE: The sun's shining.

MORGENHALL: Can we go?

FOWLE: I think the door's been open some time. (*He tries it. It is unbolted and swings open.*) After you, Mr. Morgenhall, please.

MORGENHALL: No, no.

FOWLE: A man of your education should go first.

MORGENHALL: I think you should lead the way, Mr. Fowle, and as your legal adviser I will follow at a discreet distance, to straighten out such little tangles as you may hope to leave in your wake. Let's go.

[*Morgenhall: whistles his fragment of tune. Fowle: his whistles join Morgenhall's. Whistling they leave the cell, Morgenhall executing, as he leaves, the steps of a small delighted dance.*]

Slow Curtain

WHAT SHALL WE TELL CAROLINE?

Michael Codron with David Hall (for Talbot Productions Ltd.) presented *What Shall We Tell Caroline?* in a double bill (with *The Dock Brief*) at the Lyric Opera House, Hammersmith, on April 9, 1958, and on May 20, 1958 at the Garrick Theatre. The cast was as follows:

LILY LOUDON ('BIN')	*Brenda Bruce*
ARTHUR LOUDON	*Maurice Denham*
TONY PETERS	*Michael Hordern*
CAROLINE	*Marianne Benet*

Directed by Stuart Burge
Designed by Disley Jones

The play was transferred to the Garrick Theatre on May 20, 1958.

Scene One

The Loudon's living room at " Highland Close School "
Coldsands. It is an extremely dilapidated room given an air
of festivity, as the curtain rises, by the fact that a table is
set for four and there are candles in odd candlesticks—one
expensive silver, the other a china " Present from
Coldsands " on the table. Doors on each side of the room,
one, left, is covered in green baize and has pinned on it a
few yellowing curling notices and charts of lessons which
haven't been read for years. The door is closed and leads to
the boys' part of the house. The door on the right is open
and light floods through it from a staircase which leads to
the bedrooms. Another door backstage right leads to the
kitchen. At the back of the room tall French windows,
which have never shut properly and let in winds of icy
severity, open on to a strip of grey asphalt, the white end
of a flag pole and the gun-metal sky of an early evening in
March.

Other furniture : a basket-work chair, a fireplace full of
paper, a very small electric fire, a horse-hair sofa wounded
and bleeding its stuffing; a roll top desk out of which bills,
writs, exercise books and reports are perpetually being
shaken by the draughts like the leaves of a dead tree. On
top of the desk there is a ukelele and a globe. Among faded
photographs of various teams an oar is hanging on the wall.

As the curtain rises Lily Loudon has her back to the
audience and is tugging at one of the drawers. As she tugs
the drawer comes right out and the globe falls down with a
sickening crash.

The crash is immediately followed by a roar from the lit
door which leads to the bedrooms. It is the voice of a small
man entirely consumed with rage.

63

ARTHUR (*off*): Imbecile!

[*Lily picks up the globe with great calmness and puts it back on the desk, thoughtfully spinning it to find England.*]

(*Off*): Lunatic! Fool! Whatever have you ruined now! What's broken! Go on. Don't keep it from me! Confess!

[*Lily picks up the drawer and carries it towards the table. She is an untidy woman, once inconspicuously good looking, whose face now wears an expression of puzzled contentment. She is wearing a lace evening dress of the late thirties, a number of straps are showing on her pale shoulders and a cigarette is dangling from a corner of her mouth. She shows no reaction at all to the diatribe from off stage.*]

ARTHUR (*off*): Just try and picture me. Stuck up here. Listening, always listening while you systematically destroy. . . .

[*Lily puts the drawer down on the table and knocks off a glass.*]

(*Off*): Aaah. What was that? The last of my dead mother's crockery? Speak up. Put me out of my agony. For pity's sake . . . the suspense. . . . What was it you imbecile? Side plate—dinner plate—not. . . . You're not to be trusted on your own. . . .]

[*Lily takes out a number of presents wrapped in bright paper and tied with ribbon and arranges them on the table. . . .*]

(*Off*): Where are they? You've hidden them again?

[*Lily smiles to herself. Carefully puts out her cigarette.*]

(*Off*): Do you realize what the time is?

[*Lily shakes her head.*]

ARTHUR (*off*): Dusk. Have you done it? Answer me, can't you? The loneliness—of getting dressed.

[*Lily puts a parcel by the place laid in the centre of the table. Arthur erupts into the room. He is a small, bristly, furiously angry man. He is wearing the trousers only of a merciless tweed suit, no collar and his braces are hanging down his back.*]

(*His anger becoming plaintive*): You can't imagine what a fly you are in the ointment of any little ceremony like this. . . . How you take the edge off my pleasure in any small moment of celebration. My own daughter's birthday. A thing I've been keenly looking forward to and you deliberately . . . hide . . . my . . . clothes.

[*Lily puts the drawer, empty now, back in the desk and comes back to face her husband.*]

Perhaps it's a mental kink in you. Is that the excuse you'd make? Do you plead insanity? If I had a pound for every time you've taken a collar stud and . . . I don't know—eaten it . . . rolled it under the chest of drawers. Now, to carefully conceal the club braces. . . . The sort of kink that makes women pinch things in Woolworths. Itching, destructive fingers. Furtive little pickers.

[*Lily pulls his braces, which are hanging down the back of his trousers up across his shoulders, and fastens them. Then she kisses his forehead. This quietens him for a moment. Then he bursts out again.*]

That's hardly the point. It's dusk.

[*He runs to the windows and throws them open. A wind, howling in, makes the candles flicker. Arthur is hauling down the flag.*]

LILY: It's bitterly cold.

ARTHUR: Found your tongue at last?

LILY: I said, it's bitterly cold.

ARTHUR (*comes back into the room, the Union Jack bundled in his arms. He kicks the windows shut behind him*): Of course it's bitterly cold. That wind's come a long way. All the way from the Ural mountains. An uninterrupted journey.

LILY: Yes, I know.

ARTHUR (*folding up the flags—calm for the moment*): Think of that. From Moscow and Vitebsk. The marshes of Poland. The flats of Prussia. The dykes of Belgium and Holland. All the way to Yarmouth. Just think of it. Flat as a playground. That's what I tell the boys.

LILY: I know you do.

ARTHUR: It's a geographical miracle. It makes this place so ideal for schooling boys. There's nothing like a wind from the Ural Mountains, Bin, for keeping boys pure in heart.

LILY: I suppose not.

ARTHUR: Added to which it kills bugs.

LILY: Yes, of course.

ARTHUR: Bugs and unsuitable thoughts. You know

66

that, Bin. You're in charge of that side of it. Have we had a single epidemic this year?

LILY: They cough in the night time. (*She is arranging the presents on the table.*) Like sheep.

ARTHUR: Colds admitted. Infectious diseases not. I had a letter only the other day. A school in Torquay. Malaria. Decimated the boys. Brought on by the relaxing climate. Thank heavens, Bin, for our exposed position.

LILY: Yes, dear.

ARTHUR: For heaven's sake don't complain about the wind, then. It gets on the nerves of a saint. To have you always carping at the wind. Think of it— one little mountain range between here and Moscow and the boys might all go down with malaria.

LILY: I wonder if Caroline's going to like her presents?

ARTHUR: Like her presents? Of course she's going to like her presents. Doesn't she always like her presents?

LILY: I only wondered. . . .

ARTHUR: If you set out to make her dissatisfied. If you sow the seeds of doubt in her young mind. . . . If you deliberately undertake to puzzle and bewilder a young girl with your extraordinary ideas of what a present *ought* to be. If you carp and criticize. . . .

LILY: I only wondered . . . if she wasn't getting on a bit for Halma.

ARTHUR: You wondered? Caroline takes it for granted. Every year she'll get her Halma and every year you'll lose three or four of her men. . . . Swallow them up like collar studs. Of course she likes Halma, you've seen her in the evenings playing it with. . . .

[*He puts the folded flag on top of the desk. Then shouts as he picks up the ukulele.*]

ARTHUR: He was here again last night!

LILY: Who?

ARTHUR: Tony Peters.

LILY: He's been here for eighteen years.

ARTHUR: But this wasn't here yesterday. He's been lurking about when I didn't know. *Singing* to you.

[*Lily smiles complacently downwards. Arthur shouts and holds out the ukulele. She takes it and holds it as if to play it. She stands still in the attitude of someone about to play the ukulele during the ensuing dialogue. The French windows open and Tony Peters enters. He is tall, debonair, and gay, although balding, with the cuffs of his blazer slightly fraying, his suede shoes shiny and his grey flannel trousers faded. He is carrying a string bag full of screw top bottles of light ale.*]

TONY: It's bloody cold.

ARTHUR: It's you.

TONY: Of course it's me. Look here, old man. Aren't you going to dress? I mean it is Caroline's birthday.

ARTHUR: Oh my God. How far can I be goaded?

TONY (*unloads his bag, sets the bottles out on the table and then throws it on top of the Union Jack*): I don't know. It's amusing to find out.

ARTHUR: You were here last night?

TONY: Certainly.

ARTHUR: Singing to Bin?

TONY: Keeping her company while you gave, to those few unlucky boys whose temperatures are still normal and who can still breathe through their noses, your usual Sunday evening sermon on " Life as a stiff row from Putney to Mortlake."

ARTHUR: So you chose that as a moment for singing . . . to a married woman.

TONY: She sat in your chair, Arthur. We turned out

68

the lights. The room was softly lit by the one bar of the electric fire. I was cross-legged on the floor. In the half-light I appeared boyish and irresistible. Lily needs no concealed lighting to look perpetually young. From under all the doors and through the cracks of the windows the wind sneered at us from Moscow—but we didn't feel the cold. In the distance we heard you say that it is particularly under Hammersmith Bridge that God requires ten hard pulls on the oar. Above us the coughs crackled like distant gunfire. My fingers cramped by the cold, I struck at my instrument. (*He takes the ukulele from Lily and plays.*)

(*Singing*)   " Oh the Captain's name
             Was Captain Brown,
             And he played his ukulele
             As the ship went down. . . ."

ARTHUR: That idiotic song.
TONY (*singing very close to Arthur*):
             " Then he bought himself
             A bar of soap,
             And washed himself
             Ashore."

[*Lily puts her hand flat over her mouth like a child to stifle her giggles.*]

ARTHUR: If either of you had the slightest idea of loyalty. If you had a grain of respect for me, for Sunday evening, for decent, wholesome living.
TONY (*singing*):
             "Oh we left her baby on the shore,
             A thing that we've never done before."

ARTHUR: It's obscene.

TONY: Obscene?

ARTHUR: Perhaps not the words. The dirty expression you put into it. When I'm not looking.

TONY (*singing*): "If you see the mother
　　　　　　Tell her gently
　　　　　　That we left her baby on the shore."

[*The giggles explode past Lily's hand.*]

ARTHUR: Bin!

LILY: I'm sorry. It just gets me every time. Poor baby. It's so damned casual.

ARTHUR: It doesn't seem to me a subject for joking.

LILY: But the way Tony sings it. Just as if he'd forgotten a baby.

ARTHUR: He probably has.

LILY: What can you be saying?

ARTHUR: I don't know. How can I know anything? Everything goes on when I'm not there. Furniture falls to the ground. This man sings. Crockery breaks. You pull his ears, stroke his hair as he squats there in front of you. Don't think I've got no imagination. I've got a vivid imagination. And my hearing is keen. Remember that. I warn you both. My hearing is exceptionally keen.

TONY: Hear that Lily? Stroke my hair more quietly in future.

[*As Arthur seems about to hit him a clock groans and strikes off stage.*]

LILY: Arthur. You must get dressed. It's nearly time. Caroline'll be down.

ARTHUR: Let her come down. It's time she found out something. Let her find out the lying and deceit and infidelity that all these years . . . let her find out that her mother spends musical evenings breathing down the neck of an ex-night club gigolo, lounge lizard, wallflower, sensitive plant, clinging vine, baby leaving, guitar twanging, Mayfair playboy, good-time Charlie, fly-by-night, moonlight flit, who can't even do quadratic equations. Let her find out all she is. Poor girl. Poor child. You're right Bin—you've brought it on us all. She's too old for Halma now.

[*He sits down exhausted. They look at him in horror. He, too, is a little horrified by what he has said.*]

TONY: Arthur. Look here, my dear old fellow. It's Caroline's party. You wouldn't spoil a party?
ARTHUR: I don't know that I feel particularly festive.
LILY: Come on, Arthur. You know how you enjoy Caroline's birthday.
ARTHUR: I always have. Up to now. Ever since she was born.
TONY: And look Arthur, my dear old Head. I bought these for us in the pub. A whiff each after dinner.

[*He takes two battered cigars out of his breast pocket.*]

ARTHUR (*crackles and smells the cigar*): That was thoughtful of you, Peters.
TONY: I know you don't smoke them as often as one might like. Only when something a little bit festive arises from time to time.
LILY (*ecstatic*): Oh Tony Peters. Beautifully managed.
ARTHUR: Perhaps my suspicions are unfounded.

LILY: You manage him so beautifully.

TONY: Why not finish dressing, my fine old head-master? Let us both face the fact, you must be bitterly cold.

ARTHUR (*starts to work himself up again*): I tell you I never feel cold. Anyway it's never cold here. Only occasionally a little brisk after sunset. Anyway who's old? Didn't you tell me, Tony Peters, that in your prep school the Third Eleven Match play was once stopped by a Zeppelin. You didn't mean to let that slide out did you? What does that make you? Pretty long in bottle for a junior assistant? Ha! Ha!

TONY: I'm not a junior assistant.

ARTHUR: What are you then?

TONY: A senior assistant.

ARTHUR: You're the only assistant. I think of you as junior.

TONY (*shrugging his shoulders*): It's a fact. I give an impression of perpetual youth. (*He slaps his pocket, brings out a half-bottle of whisky.*) I thought this might slip down well with the whiffs.

ARTHUR (*mollified*): It looks like good stuff.

TONY: I've always had an eye for a piece of good stuff.

[*Arthur looks up suspiciously.*]

TONY: Arthur, Head, do believe me. That remark was in no way meant to be offensive.

ARTHUR: I'll take your word for it.

LILY: So hurry on Arthur do. We must be just so for when Caroline comes in.

TONY: Go on Head. Spick and span. That's the order of the day. Look, Lily's in her best. As always, on these occasions.

[*Lily and Tony pat him, steer him towards the door; he turns to them before he goes out.*]

ARTHUR: For God's sake, you two. Use your imaginations. Think what it's like being up there, wrestling with a collar in utter ignorance. Tormented. . . .

TONY: Get a start on the collar now. You'll be back with us in five minutes.

ARTHUR: Five minutes? Haven't you ever thought, Peters, the whole course of a man's life can be changed in five minutes. Does it take five minutes to die? Or catch malaria? Or say the one word to unhinge another man's wife from him? All right, I'll trust you. But look here, both. No singing. Don't torture me with that.

TONY: If I do sing, I'll sing so quietly that no human ear could ever pick it up. I'll sing in notes only audible to a dog.

ARTHUR: That's worse.

LILY: Now go on, really. Caroline can't sit and gaze at a brass collar stud on her birthday.

ARTHUR: I'm going. For Caroline's sake, I'm going. Poor child. (*He stands in the doorway, the door open.*)

TONY: For Caroline's sake. Goodbye.

[*Tony shuts the door on him. Then walks over to the basket work chair and drops into it.*]

TONY: He's not right.
LILY: About what?
TONY: About me.
LILY: What about you?
TONY: I *can* do quadratic equations.
LILY: Another year gone. Another birthday come again.

73

TONY: Gather all the Xs and Ys on to one side.

LILY: Eighteen years old. (*She fiddles with the presents.*)

TONY: Remove the brackets.

LILY: Oh Tony, can she possibly be happy?

TONY: Remember that minus times minus makes plus.

LILY: Tony can you hear me?

TONY: As an example. In the problem, if it takes ten barbers twenty minutes at double speed to shave " y " tramps let " x " equal the time taken to shave half a tramp. That's Arthur's problem. Arthur can *teach* quadratics all right. But can he *do* them. Isn't that rather the point?

LILY: Everyone here is so taken up with their own concerns.

TONY: I'm sorry.

LILY: I quite understand. You're naturally anxious for your algebra.

TONY: No, Lily. Not at all. Come and sit down.

LILY: Where?

TONY: Here. (*He slaps his knee.*)

LILY: I'd be taking a risk.

TONY: All we can take in this mean, tight-fisted world.

[*She giggles and sits on the floor in front of him, her elbows on his knees, gazing up at him.*]

LILY: Now is Caroline. . . .

TONY: What?

LILY: Happy.

TONY: She shows no signs of being otherwise.

LILY (*looks down suddenly. Her eyes full of tears*): How can she tell us?

TONY: Poor Arthur. It may not be so bad as he thinks.

74

LILY: When it's something we must have all noticed why don't we discuss. . . .

TONY: At first perhaps, it was our headmaster's fault. When it happened at first I blamed him. But since last birthday I've begun to suspect. . . .

LILY: Tony. You're talking about it. About Caroline. . . .

TONY (*talking quickly as if to avoid an awkward moment*): Caroline is now eighteen which must mean that she was born in 1940. Dark days with storm clouds hanging over Europe. Poor child she never knew the pre-war when you could week-end in Paris on a two-pound ten note and get a reasonable packet of cigarettes for elevenpence complete with card which could be collected towards a jolly acceptable free gift. She never borrowed a bus and took a couple of girls from Elstree Studio out dancing up the Great West Road and home with the milk and change left out of a pound.

[*Lily begins to smile up at him.*]

LILY: It's yourself you're discussing.

TONY: She missed the Big Apple and the Lambeth Walk and the Palais Glide. She couldn't even come to the party I gave for the Jubilee. Poor child, God knows I'd have invited her. Twenty-three of us in a line gliding down the Earl's Court Road at three in the morning. Smooth as skaters. (*Takes up his ukelele and sings*)

> "She was sweet sixteen.
> On the village green.
> Poor little Angeline."

ARTHUR (*off stage shouting*): For pity's sake.

[*Tony shrugs his shoulders and puts his ukelele down, exasperated.*]

TONY: Really. He's like my old landlady in the Earls Court Road. Bump on the ceiling with a broom if you so much as lifted a girl from the floor to the sofa.

LILY (*elbows on his knees*): Was it so carefree for you then, in Earl's Court?

TONY (*modestly*): Carefree? Look Lily, I knew ten clubs where the drummers were happy to allow me a whirl with their sticks. I knew twenty pubs in S.W. alone which were flattered to take my cheque, and as for the opposite sex....

[*Lily looks up at him admiringly.*]

I had enough telephone numbers to fill a reasonably bulky pocket diary from January to Christmas. Even the little space for my weight and size of hat, Lily, was crammed with those available numbers.

LILY: What do you think took away all our happy days?

TONY: Are they gone?

LILY: Arthur says so. Driven away, he says, by the Russians and the Socialists and the shocking way they've put up the rates.

TONY: We can still have a good time.

LILY: But can Caroline? If she could only tell....

[*She gets up and wanders to the table, arranging the presents.*]

TONY: Well there....

LILY: And when she never knew....

TONY: Isn't that rather the point?

LILY: Deprived, Tony, of all the pre-war we ever had?

TONY: All that pre-war denied her.

LILY: What would become of us, do you suppose, if we hadn't got that pre-war to think about?

TONY (*he gets up from the chair and stands with his arm round her shoulders*): It's not all over. We don't just let it die out.

LILY: It mustn't.

TONY: We keep it going you see. And it keeps us going too.

[*Pause, as they stand side by side.*]

ARTHUR (*yelling from off stage*): What have you two got to be so damned *quiet* about?

[*They smile at each other and Tony breaks away from her and walks round the room rubbing his hands and flapping his arms. He begins to talk in the clipped, stoical voice of an explorer reminiscing.*]

TONY: The glass stood at forty below when we unpacked our Christmas dinner in Camp A. (*He blows on his nails*).

LILY (*thoughtfully, softly*): I remember the day you arrived. It was summer and Arthur was out taking Cricket practice.

TONY: Frozen penguin and a mince pie which my dear sister had sent from Godalming, found, quite by chance, stuffed in a corner of my flea-bag.

LILY: I heard the sound of your two-seater on the gravel.

TONY: We broke the mince pie with our ice axes. Three dogs died in the night.

LILY: Why did you have to sell that two-seater?

TONY: . . . Prayed to God before sharing our penguin. Now a thousand miles from base camp. Had a premonition we should never see England again. . . .

LILY: I was alone in the middle of the afternoon. I heard you singing outside the window. It opened and you came in. . . . When you saw me standing all alone. . . .

TONY: Peters. . . .

LILY: Yes?

TONY: With silent heroism. . . .

LILY: What?

TONY: Walked out of the tent.

[*With a dramatic gesture he steps behind the curtain of the French window and is lost to sight.*]

LILY (*standing alone centre stage, her arms extended. A slight wait*): Tony! Why won't you ever be serious with me?

[*Arthur enters, fully dressed, his hair brushed and shining*].

ARTHUR: Where the hell's he got to now?

[*Lily makes a gesture of despair.*]

ARTHUR: It's no use lying, Bin. I can see his filthy suede shoes under the curtain.

[*He pulls the curtain aside. Tony smiles at him, pats his shoulder and walks out into the room. Tony lights a cigarette with great finesse. Arthur sits down at the table, raises his hands as if to say something several times. The words don't exist for what he feels that he must say.*]

TONY: Now Arthur. Don't make a fool of yourself over this.

ARTHUR: I ... make a fool?

TONY: It's quite reasonable.

LILY: Tony, it seems, was discovering the North Pole.

ARTHUR: The North Pole?

TONY: Shut your eyes, Headmaster, and what can you hear? The ice cracking like gun fire in the distance. The wind howling in the guy ropes. The fizz of the solid fuel as it melts a little snow for your evening cocoa.

ARTHUR: Oh my God! (*He buries his face in his hands.*)

LILY (*laughing*): Give the poor man a little peace.

TONY: Peace? What does Arthur want with peace? He'd be as bored as a retired General with nothing to do but keep chickens and explore the possibility of life after death. As lonely as a bull without a bull fighter. As hard up for conversation as an invalid without his malignant growth. Give him peace and you'd bury your husband. What can he listen to in this great frozen institution except the sound of his own eternal irritation? (*He claps him on the shoulder.*) Keep going, Headmaster, go off every minute. You're the dear old fog horn that lets us know we're still afloat.

LILY: Ssh. Caroline!

[*Arthur has raised his two clenched fists and now opens his hands and pushes himself up from the table.*]

ARTHUR: She's been out for a walk.

[*Caroline has come in through the French window halfway through Tony's speech. Now she closes them and comes into*

79

the room, crosses it, and hangs her mackintosh on the back of the door that leads to the school.]

(*Pulling out his watch and looking at it.*) She usually does at this time.

[*Caroline comes up to the three of them, and looks at them without expression. She sits down. The others stand. She is eighteen and extremely beautiful, her beauty being such that it is strange, composed and vaguely alarming. She has a look of complete innocence and wears, unexpectedly, the sort of clothes worn by starlets on the covers of very cheap film magazines. These clothes have an appearance of being home made. She does not speak. While she is on the stage the other characters speak faster as if to conceal the fact of her silence from themselves.*]

TONY: I wonder where she's been?
LILY: Usually along the front.
TONY: She doesn't feel the cold?
ARTHUR: Brought up here, of course she doesn't notice it.
TONY: She always walks alone?
LILY: Hardly ever picks up a friend.

[*Pause while they all think of something to say. Caroline is still expressionless.*]

ARTHUR: Well—she's back just in time.
TONY: Haven't you got something to say to her?
ARTHUR: You needn't remind me. Many happy returns of the day.

[*He puts his hand out. Caroline shakes it. Arthur sits down at the table.*]

TONY: Many, many, happies, Caroline dear. (*He stoops to kiss the top of her head.*)

[*Caroline lifts her face and kisses him on the mouth. She is still expressionless. He sits down, disconcerted, patting his lips with his handkerchief.*]

LILY: Caroline, my baby. Don't grow up any more.

[*Lily hugs Caroline like a child and then sits down.*]

ARTHUR: She didn't like you saying that.
TONY: She didn't mind.

[*Pause while Lily begins to cry.*]

ARTHUR (*suddenly loses his temper*): Will you provoke me, Bin, with these bloody waterworks?
TONY: Look. She hasn't noticed her presents yet.
ARTHUR: She was upset.
TONY: No she wasn't.

[*Caroline looks down at her place and lifts her hands in amazement. Her face is still without expression.*]

LILY (*recovering*): She's seen them now.
ARTHUR (*eagerly*): She may open mine first.
TONY: Well, of all the selfish. . . .
ARTHUR: She's going to. I hope you didn't notice me buying it, Caroline, in the High Street yesterday. Creeping out of W. H. Smith's.
TONY: Now you've given the game away.
ARTHUR: What are you hinting?
TONY: The mention of W. H. Smith. Now she can rule out stockings or underwear or any nice toilet water.

[*Caroline shakes the parcel.*]

TONY: Now she's guessed what it is.
ARTHUR: I don't believe she has.

[*Caroline shakes her head.*]

ARTHUR: No, she hasn't.

[*Caroline opens the parcel, it contains a Halma set and three boy's adventure books.*]

TONY: Same old things. She's bored with Halma.
ARTHUR: No she's not.
TONY: Yes she is.
ARTHUR: Anyway it's a wholesome game, Peters, unlike the indoor sports you're addicted to.
TONY: And these books. You only buy them to read them yourself. Three midshipmen stranded on a desert island. (*Picks up one and starts to read.*) "Give over tickling, Harry, giggled his chum, little guessing it was the hairy baboon that had crept up behind the unsuspecting youngsters. . . ."
ARTHUR: She appreciates it.
LILY (*soothingly*): Of course she does, don't let's quarrel. Not on the birthday.
TONY (*putting down the book*): I suppose it takes all tastes.
LILY: Perhaps now she'll open mine.

[*Caroline picks up a parcel.*]

LILY: I made it for you, dear. It took so long. It seem to have been making it all my life.

[*Caroline opens the parcel. A long sweater, white and endless with the school colours at the neck. She holds it in front of herself. It's far too long.*]

LILY: Oh Caroline. There's too much of it. I had far too much spare time.

TONY (*putting his hand on Lily's shoulder*): She likes it. She thinks it'll keep her warm.

ARTHUR: Warm? Keep her warm did you say? I tell you it's perfectly warm here, all the year round.

TONY: There now, Headmaster. Lily's right. We shouldn't quarrel on the birthday. And look. She's knitted in the school colours. That'll cheer you up, you know. When you see those colours always round your daughter.

ARTHUR: At least it shows some sense of loyalty.

TONY: Of course, not being, strictly speaking, a parent my present, gets opened last.

ARTHUR (*resentfully*): A treat saved up for you.

[*Caroline picks up Tony's present. Holds it against her cheek. Listens to it.*]

TONY: I believe.... Yes. I think I am right in saying (*radio commentator's voice*). "The ceremony is just about to begin. It's a wonderful spectacle here to-day. The Lady Mayoress has released the pigeons. The massed bands are striking up. The Boy Scouts are fainting in unprecedented numbers and...."

[*Caroline undoes the parcel, produces a gilt powder compact*].

ARTHUR: What can it be?

[*Caroline opens the compact and sprinkles powder on her nose.*]

LILY: My baby....

ARTHUR: Take that muck off your face. I forbid it. Go straight upstairs and wash.

TONY: Headmaster!

LILY: Surely Tony. She's still too young.

[*Tony goes behind Caroline, his hands on each side of her head he directs her face to one parent, then another.*]

TONY: Can you be such unobservant parents? Your daughter has now been using cosmetics in considerable quantities for many years.

ARTHUR: Is this true, Bin?

LILY: She's still a child.

TONY: Her table upstairs is covered with tubes, little brushes and the feet of rabbits. In an afternoon, with nothing better to do, she can turn from a pale, coal eyed, fourteenth wife of an oil sheik to a brash, healthy, dog-keeping, pony-riding, daddy-adoring virgin with a pillar box mouth. Her beauty spots come off on the face towels and when she cries she cries black tears.

ARTHUR: Your appalling influence.

TONY: The passage of time, Headmaster. What can you and I do to prevent it?

ARTHUR: I see her as a little girl.

TONY: Then you don't bother to look.

ARTHUR: Did *you* notice Bin?

LILY: When the sun falls straight on her I do have my suspicions. We've had so little sun lately.

[*The clock groans and strikes. Caroline puts down the powder compact and goes out of the room, through the door to the boys' department.*]

She's gone.

TONY: To collect her presents from the boys.

ARTHUR: Of course. I was forgetting.

TONY: She always does that next. Then she comes back to show us what they've given.

ARTHUR: Of course. . . . of course.

[*Arthur and Lily are staring thoughtfully in front of them. Tony walks about nervously, about to broach a difficult subject.*]

TONY: My old friends. (*He gets no reaction and starts again*) Colleagues. Of course I'm not a parent.

ARTHUR (*angrily*): If only I could be sure of that.

TONY (*smiling, flattered*): Not in any official sense. But I have at least been a child.

LILY (*looking at him affectionately*): Yes, Tony, of course you have.

TONY: Now frankly speaking, isn't eighteen a bit of a cross roads? Isn't there something, can't you feel, that Caroline ought to be told?

ARTHUR: Told?

TONY: Yes.

LILY: What sort of thing, Tony, had you in mind?

TONY (*suddenly at a loss*): We must have *something* to tell her. At least I should have thought so. Nothing to embarass any one to tell, of course. . . . But (*more positive*) . . . her *education*. Aren't there a few gaps there?

ARTHUR: You don't find everything in the covers of books, Peters. That's why I always lay the emphasis on organized games.

TONY: Yes. I noticed. (*He picks up his ukelele and begins to play odd notes, tuning it as he speaks, more vaguely and with less assurance.*)

[*Lily goes out and, during Tony's speech, comes back with a tray, including a dish of sausages and mash which she puts down to keep warm by the electric fire.*]

It's not that I'm all that keen on education myself. In fact I merely drifted into it. It was a thé dansant on the river, Maidenhead. The waiter was feeding the swans, he had an apron full of bread crumbs. I was dancing with a girl called Fay Knockbroker. She was so small and yellow and it was hot to touch her. Like a red hot buttercup.

[*Arthur makes an explosion of disgust. Lily looks up at him from the dishes and smiles and goes out again.*]

. . . . Tony, she said, Why don't you do something? Why don't you work? It appeared her father Knockbroker, what did he deal in, taps?—I really forget, had said marriage was forbidden unless I worked. I had five shillings in my trousers that afternoon. I couldn't have covered the cucumber sandwiches.

ARTHUR: Grossly irresponsible.

TONY: In fact marriage, was far from my thoughts. I only wanted to get Fay launched in a punt and pushed out under the willows.

ARTHUR: Disgusting.

TONY: Probably. But it's that punt, those willows, that have kept me going in all our cold winters.

[*Lily comes in again with the tomato ketchup.*]

That and. . . .

ARTHUR: Don't say it! I can guess. . . .

TONY: How do you live, Headmaster, without any of those old past moments to warm you up?

ARTHUR: I have my memories. A cry from the mega-phone on the tow path. A cheer under Barnes Bridge.

TONY: But Miss Knockbroker wasn't stepping on board that afternoon. You get a job, she said, or I stay on dry land and marry Humphrey Ewart. He works!

ARTHUR (*interested, grudgingly*): Did he?

TONY: She met him at the Guards' Boat Club. Blow-ing safes turned out to be his profession. Knock-broker was very livid when it all came out after the marriage.

ARTHUR: And you?

TONY: I went up to London to get a job. I had to leave her to pay for tea. What could I do? I didn't know anything. I had to teach. I had no great en-thusiasm for education. I might have come to love it. As tutor cramming a young millionaire in the South of France, with his widowed mother bringing us long pink drinks to wash down the logarithms....

ARTHUR (*suddenly roaring with laughter*): And you ended out here!

TONY: I only came temporarily. Till something else offered.

ARTHUR: You are still temporary. As far as I'm concerned.

LILY: You don't regret it Tony?

TONY (*looking round at her, then brassly.*): Of course not. No regrets. I've no enthusiasm for education. But I can't help thinking. There are things Caroline should be *told*.

ARTHUR: What for instance?

TONY: We've had experience of life.

LILY (*lovingly*): Ah yes. How very true. Great experience of life.

TONY: Now, shouldn't we be passing on that ex-perience to her?

ARTHUR: I'm against passing on experience. Boys find it very embarrassing.

TONY: But Caroline, Headmaster, isn't this rather the point we have to face? Is not, and can never be, barring all accidents, a boy.

ARTHUR: The principle's the same. I have it so often in class. You start by telling them something unimportant like the date of the Spanish Armada, 1585.

TONY: 1582.

ARTHUR: 1585.

TONY: 1582.

ARTHUR: Fifteen hundred and eighty five. The year of our Lord.

LILY: What can it matter after all these years?

ARTHUR: Imbecile. Don't interrupt me. Of course it matters. It's the mental discipline.

TONY: All right, Headmaster. Have it your own way. 1585.

ARTHUR: 1585. You start to tell them. . . . The Battle of the Armada. When England's Virgin Queen. . . . Then you've laid yourself open. . . .

TONY (*imitating*): Sir! What's a virgin?

ARTHUR: You see! It's most undesirable. The lesson may have half an hour to go, and if you start telling them about virgins where will you be when it's time to ring the bell? Know what I do Peters, if any questions of that type comes up?

TONY: Yes. I do.

ARTHUR: I run straight out of the room and ring the bell myself. And that's my advice to you.

LILY: I suppose it's natural for them, to be curious.

TONY: They don't ask any questions unless they already know the answers.

[*Arthur gets up and walks about, gradually working himself into a rage again.*]

ARTHUR: That's purely cynical. Their minds are delightfully blank. That's how it's got to stay, it's the only way for Caroline. You start it, Peters. You feed her with bits of geography and history and mathematics. What comes next? Little scraps of information from you about Maidenhead and the Earls Court Road. Little tips from Bin on how to make love to another man while your husband's upstairs dressing. Little hints from both of you about face powder and silk stockings, free love and Queen Elizabeth and birth control and decimals and vulgar fractions and punts under the willow trees and she'll be down the slope—woosh! on the toboggan and you'll never stop her until she crashes into the great black iron railings of the answer which, please God, she mustn't ever know.

TONY: Which one is that?

ARTHUR: That ever since you came here and met Caroline's mother this decent school has been turned into a brothel. A corrupt. . . .

[He stops at the sound of a baby crying off stage.]

What ever?

[The baby cries again.]

LILY (*delighted*): A baby crying.

TONY: One of the boys has asked the right question at last.

[Caroline wanders in from the boys' door, her arms full of jokes. She stops by Arthur and hands him the cardboard box which, when she turns it upside down, cries like a baby. Arthur turns it and it yells. He slowly relaxes.]

LILY: It's just a joke. . . .

TONY: One of her presents from the boys.

ARTHUR: How very, very amusing.

TONY: How strange these boys are.

[*Caroline hands Tony a bottle of beer. He tries to open it and finds it's made of rubber. Lily gets a squeaking banana. Caroline has a pair of glasses which include a nose and teeth which she puts on. They all sit down, Caroline quite motionless in her false nose, the others urgently talking.*]

TONY: Will you light the candles, Headmaster? Give a warm, shaded, Café Royal touch to the proceedings.

ARTHUR (*lighting the candles*): Sausages and mash I see.

LILY (*serving it out*): And red jelly to follow.

ARTHUR: Always Caroline's favourite menu.

TONY: Since she was twelve.

ARTHUR: That's why we always put it on for the birthday.

LILY: It marks the occasion.

ARTHUR: When I was a boy my birthday always fell when I was away from home at Cadet camp. My old aunt gave me my cake to take in a tin. I had to keep it under my camp bed until the day came, then I'd get it out and eat it.

LILY: Let's be grateful. Caroline doesn't have to go to Cadet camp. She can birthday at home.

ARTHUR: As often as not when I came to open that tin the bird had flown.

TONY: Poor old Headmaster. I never knew that about you.

ARTHUR: Odd thing about it. I suspected that chaplain.

TONY: Not of scoffing your cake?

ARTHUR: It's a fact. I couldn't get it out of my head.

An effiminate sort of fellow, the chaplain. Welsh. And he had a sweet tooth.

LILY: I'm giving Caroline some more because it's her favourite dinner.

TONY: Yes. I see.

ARTHUR: It was terribly upsetting for a young boy in my position.

TONY: Indeed yes.

ARTHUR: You can't put your heart into Church Parade when you suspect the padre of nibbling at your one and only birthday present.

TONY: Let's hope you misjudged him.

ARTHUR: I was a sound judge of character. He was a man who let the side down badly.

TONY: Suspicious of everyone. Even then.

ARTHUR: What are you trying to infer?

TONY: Nothing at all. Shall I do the honours again, Headmaster?

ARTHUR: Yes. And when you come to Caroline's glass.

TONY: What?

ARTHUR: Fill it up.

LILY: With alcohol? She won't like it.

[*Tony fills Caroline's glass. She drains it thirstily.*]

TONY: There, Lily. It appears you were wrong.

ARTHUR: Thinking it over, Peters, I have thought your earlier remarks weren't entirely senseless. Caroline *has* reached a turning point. The time has come when she can be invited to join her father and mother in a light stimulant. It's a privilege, and like all privileges it brings new responsibilities.

TONY: In my humble opinion there are very few responsibilities involved in a glass of beer.

ARTHUR: There are responsibilities in everything, running a school, getting married, living at all. That's what we've got to tell Caroline. She's got to have faith in something bigger than herself.

LILY: Caroline's a woman now. Isn't that right, Tony? Didn't you say that?

TONY: Almost a woman, I should say.

LILY: Then surely there are things only a woman can tell her?

ARTHUR: There are bigger things in life than knitting patterns and . . . bottling fruit.

I mean there *are* things a person can sacrifice himself for. The side. The school. The right comrades, sweating at the oar.

TONY: There speaks the cox of the West Woolwich rowing club.

ARTHUR: Will you mock everything Peters?

TONY: The small man yelling through a paper megaphone while the comrades lug themselves to death at forty from fatty degeneration of the heart.

ARTHUR: Is nothing to be sacred?

TONY: There are better ways of getting heart failure.

ARTHUR: It all comes down to *that*.

TONY: Caroline's young. Every day she should collect some small pleasure, to keep her warm when the years begin to empty out. She should try everything, and not mind making mistakes. When she reaches our age it won't be her mistakes she'll regret. . . .

ARTHUR: What are you telling her?

TONY: When I remember those girls at Maidenhead, their thumbs up, their faces smiling, doing the Lambeth Walk. . . . It's not the ones I got away for the weekend I regret. It's the ones I never had the courage to ask.

ARTHUR: I was trying to give Caroline something

to believe in, and you will everlastingly chip in with your unsavoury reminisences. . . .

TONY: Headmaster, are we attempting too much? Suppose we just give her some accurate information. Such as . . . where Gibraltar is.

ARTHUR: Gibraltar?

TONY: Yes. Go on. Tell her.

ARTHUR: At the bottom of Spain.

TONY: The bottom?

ARTHUR: Coming round the corner. Cadiz on the right.

TONY: You mean the right?

ARTHUR: The left then. Malaga on the right. Do I mean the left?

TONY: Headmaster. Are you sure you have any information to transfer?

ARTHUR: All right Peters. (*Getting up*). You've managed it. You've cast a blight. You've had your mockery. You've sneered at the most respected club on the river. You've spoiled the birthday for me now. I'm not staying. It's no use beseeching.

TONY: But Headmaster.

ARTHUR: You've rubbed the bloom off the birthday for me. I'm leaving you two together. Remember— a child is watching.

[*He goes out, slamming the door to the bedrooms.*]

LILY: He's gone.

TONY: Yes.

[*Caroline sighs and sits down in the basket chair.*]

TONY: If only he wouldn't take it as such a personal matter. It's not my fault where they put Gibraltar. (*He picks up the ukelele and tunes it.*)

93

LILY: Ssh. Caroline's expecting a song.

TONY: An old one. . . .

LILY: That Turk and the extraordinary Russian?

TONY (*singing*):

"Oh the sons of the prophet are hardy and bold
And quite unaccustomed to fear,
But the greatest by far
In the courts of the Shah—
Was Abdul the Bul Bul Emir."

LILY: Of course Caroline adores this one. . . .

TONY: "If they wanted a man to encourage the van or shout. . . .

LILY (*shouts.*): 'Atta boy.'

TONY: In the rear
          Without any doubt
          They always sent out. . . ."

Damn. I almost forgot. I owe the pub for those whiffs. I'm duty bound to slip back.

LILY: Oh Tony.

TONY: They were an expensive gesture. . . .

LILY: Have a look in that box. The egg money. . . .

[*Tony finds five shillings in a box on the mantelpiece. Pockets it in triumph.*]

LILY: Must you go tonight?

TONY (*dramatic voice stifling sobs, tough American accent*): 'I'm only a small guy, not very brave. I guess this is just one of the things that comes on a small guy and well, he's just got to go through with it if he ever wants to be able to shake his own hand again this side of the Great River. Maybe if I go through with this Lily, hundreds of little guys all over the world are going to be safe to shake their own hands and look themselves in the whites of their eyes. Maybe if I don't they won't. Kinda hard to tell. (*Looks out of the French window.*) It's just about sun up time. Guess Arthur Loudon's boys are sawing off their shot guns 'bout now down there in the alfafa. So long folks. If ma sobers up tell her Goodbye. Let's hit the trail now. Don't forget the empties. (*He hitches up his trousers, picks up the string bag of empties and lurches out of the French window.*)

[*Lily is laughing hard. Caroline is quite impassive.*]

TONY (*off stage*): Bang, bang, bang.
LILY: Tony, you'll kill me.
TONY (*staggering in backwards, his hand on his heart*): They killed me too, honey. Tell ma I'm feeling just fine, can't hardly notice the difference. (*Looks religiously upwards.*) O.K. Mr. Gabriel Archangel. I heard you. I'm a coming. Maybe take a little time on account of this old webbed foot of mine."

[*Limps out of French window.*]

LILY: Oh Tony Peters. What should I do without you?

[*Pause.*]

Caroline, they try to tell you things—but what can they tell you? We're not men you see, we're something different. Lots of men don't realise that. All men except, except Tony.

[*Caroline still sits impassive. Lily kneels on the floor in front of her.*]

LILY: I'm a woman, Caroline. And you're going to be one as well. Nothing can stop you. I'm a woman

and what does Arthur call me? He calls me Bin.
Bin, when my name is Lily. Now does Bin sound
like a woman's name to you? You know why he
calls me Bin? Because he wants me to be his friend,
his assistant, his colleague, his thoroughly good
chap. To rough it with him on a walking tour
through life. He's said that to me, Caroline. How
can I be a good chap, I wasn't born a chap. *My sex
gets in the way.* That's why he gets so angry. (*She
gets up and moves about the room.*) Look Caroline, do
you know why he calls me Bin? Because my father
did and my uncle did and so did my five brothers
who all married soft hearted tittering girls in fluffy
pullovers which came off on them like falling hair
and white peep toe shoes and had pet names for
their hot water bottles. Those brothers called me
Bin. Good old Bin, you can put her on the back of
the motor bike. Bin's marvellous, she can go in the
dicky because her hair's always in a tangle and her
cheeks are like bricks and the wind can't do her any
harm, but Babs or Topsy or Melanie has to sit in
front because she's such a fuss pot and so I can
change gear next to her baby pink and artificial silk
and get her angora all tied up in my Harris tweed.
If you take Bin out it's for great slopping pints and
the other one about the honeymoon couple in the
French hotel, and then you can be sick in the hedge
on the way home because Bin's a good chap. We're
women Caroline. They buy us beer when we long
to order protection and flattery and excitement and
crème de menthe and little bottles of sparkling wine
with silver paper tops and oh my God, we long to be
kept warm. Aren't I right? Isn't that how we reel?
Mothers and daughters and wives. . . . (*kneeling
again.*) Oh Caroline tell me I'm right. Caroline.
Speak to us. What have we done wrong?

[*Caroline says nothing, but, for the first time she smiles slowly and puts her hands on her mother's shoulder. Lily gets up, gets the tray which she has left leaning against the wall and begins to stack the plates.*]

LILY: Anyway all my friends got married and there was only Arthur. He was small and violent and believed in everything. Life wasn't much fun at home, my brothers got married and their wives refused to take on their pets. After the youngest left I was walking out with five Alsatian dogs. Father economised on the wedding. We needn't hire a car for Bin, he said. My brother Tommy took me to the church on the back of his motor bike. My first long dress and I was rushed up to my wedding wearing goggles and waving in the wind like a flag. We're women, Caroline. There's supposed to be a mystery about us. We should be sprung on our men like a small surprise in the warmth and darkness of the night—not delivered by a boy on a motor bike like a parcel that's come undone in the post. It shouldn't be like that for you Caroline. The day after the marriage I told Arthur I loved him. There are more important things than love he said. What more important things? Companionship, he said, helping one another. Now we're dedicated, our lives are dedicated. What to? I asked him. The boys. Can you believe it? Those dreadful children coughing like old sheep upstairs. I was dedicated to *them*. I went to look at them. They were in striped pyjamas, they looked like little old convicts with cropped heads and match-stick arms and legs. They had hard, sexless voices and the faint, cold smell of lead pencils. And you know what? Arthur said it would make them think of me as more of a sport. He told them to call me Bin. I ask you. Is that a name for a woman?

ARTHUR (*shouts off stage*): What are you doing, Bin?

LILY (*suddenly shouts back*): *Clearing away.* (*Then quietly.*) That day was so empty. It seemed I'd been born a woman for nothing at all. Yet I couldn't be a man. Arthur wanted me to play cricket with the boys—can you imagine that Caroline? My legs were still young, and his idea was to see them buckled up in cricketing pads. My soft hands in the gloves of a wicket keeper. . . .

ARTHUR (*off stage shouts*): I heard singing. Then the singing stopped. What's he got round to now?

LILY: I was a woman and there was no time for me.

ARTHUR (*off stage*): Don't you realise? I went to bed because of the way you all treated me. I can't get out again. It'd be ridiculous!

LILY (*shouts*): I'll be up in a minute. (*Quiet.*) Just a succession of days. Saints' Days with no lessons before breakfast. Sundays when the boys hit each other in the evening. Mondays when Arthur loses his temper. Nothing. Like a party when no one's remembered to send out the invitation. . . . Then Tony came. . . .

[*She leaves the dishes stacked on the tray and sits near Caroline.*]

ARTHUR: Bin! Come here, Bin! Don't leave me alone.

LILY: You know Tony can never be serious. Perhaps he's not very honest. Does he speak the truth all the time? I don't care. He treats me as if I was born to be a woman. Lily, Lily, all the time and never a nickname. And he's made Arthur jealous. (*Triumphant.*) *They quarrel over me Caroline. They've been fighting over me for years.* Imagine that! Good old Bin.

98

She won't mind going home alone now we've met you girls. . . .

[*Lily gets up. Turns to the middle of the room.*]

But now it's Lily Loudon and Arthur's developed jealousy.

ARTHUR (*shouting off stage*): Are you going to rob me of my sleep? It's the semi-finals tomorrow.

LILY (*shouting*): What semi-finals?

ARTHUR (*shouting back*): Squash. Masters v Boys.

LILY (*contemptuously*): Squash! What did Tony say today? Lily, always Lily you see, needs no half light to look perpetually beautiful. He said that. A man with all those available telephone numbers.

ARTHUR (*plaintifully off*): The boys'll make a fool of me if I don't get some sleep.

LILY: It'll come to you Caroline. If you're a woman it's bound to come. In the middle of the afternoon, perhaps. During cricket practise. You'll hear a sound in the gravel, someone singing outside the window. You stand quite still holding your breath in case they should go away. And then, when the window opens. . . . Caroline, I'm telling you. It's the only thing that matters. . . .

ARTHUR (*shouts*): Am I never to see you again?

LILY: One day he'll do his insides mischief, shouting like that. Just put the tray in the kitchen would you. We'll wash up in the morning. I shouldn't have told you all that. I've enjoyed it though, telling myself. Don't remember it all. Only remember you're Caroline—make them call you that. Don't let them call you a funny name.

ARTHUR (*off stage*): Bin!

LILY: Coming Arthur. I'm coming now.

[*She looks at Caroline and then goes out of the door. Caroline sighs, stretches and then gets up and carries the tray out of the room. The stage is empty. Caroline comes back and looks round the room. She takes out her powder compact. Standing over by the mantelpiece, powders her nose. She puts out the light. The stage is dark, only the electric fire glowing. She draws the curtains in front of the French window showing a square of grey moonlight. She goes and sits down to wait. She waits. There's a footstep. She stands, her arms outstretched.*]

TONY (*off stage, singing*):

"... 'Do you hold life so dull.
   That you're seeking to end your career?'
'Vile infidel know
   You have trod on the toe....'

[*Tony comes in at the French window. Stumbles in the darkness.*]

What's up? Everyone gone to bed?

[[*Caroline makes a slight sound and falls on him, her arms round his neck, her mouth pressed on his. In the square of moonlit French window he is struggling to release his neck from her hands. When he frees himself he dashes to the door and switches on the light.*]

TONY: Caroline. What have they been telling you now?

[*She moves towards him.*]

Whatever it was—you can't have understood. You must have got it wrong.

[*He opens the door behind him. He disappears rapidly through the door. Caroline faces the audience. She is not unduly upset. Her hands turn palm outwards, she heaves a small sigh, her eyes turn upwards in mock despair. On her, the Curtain slowly falls.*]

Scene Two

Early evening, the next day. The table is laid with an assortment of tea cups and plates. Caroline is alone, reading a letter propped up on the tea pot in front of her. She looks very pleased, as she folds up the letter and puts it in a pocket of her skirt.

She gets up and goes over to the roll top desk. In wrestling to get a suitcase from behind it she knocks over the globe.

ARTHUR (*shouting off stage, from the right*): What's that for mercy's sake?

[*Caroline brings out the battered suitcase and takes it over to the hearth rug where she opens it and begins to drop in the presents which she has arranged on the mantelpiece.*]

(*shouts*): Bin. Is that you?

[*Caroline drops in the baby crier which screams in the case.*]

What are you playing at you imbecile?

[*Caroline shuts the case. Tony appears outside the French windows and starts to haul down the flag. Caroline crosses the room, and, as he comes in, hastily puts her suitcase outside the door that leads to the boys' department.*]

ARTHUR (*off*): Who is it, burglars? Answer me, Bin.
TONY (*folding up the Union Jack*): It may be a silly business but it pleases the headmaster. Caroline. I wanted to talk. Couldn't we talk. I promise you . . . I haven't slept. I believe, I feel sure . . . we could . . . both . . . talk.

[*Caroline exits through the boys' door. Arthur bursts into the room putting on his coat.*]

ARTHUR: I heard you Peters. Make no mistake about that. . . .

[*Tony folds up the Union Jack, puts it on the desk and goes over to the table, sits down and pours himself out a cup of tea. He looks very tired.*]

TONY: I've never felt it before, Headmaster. It never really took hold of me till now.

ARTHUR: Not to speak can be just as deceptive as lying, Peters. There's an awful, deceptive silence about people in this house, a goading, tormenting, blank silence. Every question I shout is like sending a soldier into the dark night of a silent, enemy country.

TONY: Have a cup of tea?

ARTHUR: Were you in here with her?

TONY: They sat in front of me, rows of boys. Usually I feel quite indifferent about them, as if they were rows of strangers sitting opposite me in a train. I merely want to avoid conversation with them until the bell rings and we can all get out at the station.

ARTHUR: What were you two doing, banging about in here? Shall I never know the truth?

TONY: Sit down and have some tea. All that shouting must leave you parched.

ARTHUR: How can I spare my voice? Leading this sort of life, I mean.

[*He sits down. Tony pours him tea.*]

TONY: It's hard for you, I do appreciate.

ARTHUR: But you're the one reason for my shouting. . . .

TONY: Let me try and explain. There they sat, these children, with the pale look of old age hanging around them—of course they're much older than us, Headmaster, you do realise that don't you?

ARTHUR: Older?

TONY: And before they are finally taken away, done up in blankets, muffled in scarves, tweed caps balanced on their ancient heads, to institutions, I felt there was something I ought to tell them. Only . . .

ARTHUR: Yes?

TONY: I couldn't for the life of me remember what it was. But if you don't tell children anything. . . .

ARTHUR: Well?

TONY: They get some extraordinary ideas.

ARTHUR: What do you mean?

TONY: I'm not sure if I'm in a position to tell you. All I can say is that I've had a shock, a pretty severe shock as it so happens, in the last twenty-four hours. I tell you, I don't often get a jolt like that these days. Last night, I say this quite frankly, sleep eluded me.

ARTHUR: Well, of course.

TONY: What do you mean, " Well of course "?

ARTHUR: Missing Bin, weren't you?

TONY: Not at the time.

ARTHUR: I winkled her away from you.

TONY: Did you now?

ARTHUR: Brought her up to bed when you least expected it.

TONY: Oh, I see.

ARTHUR: My God, I'd liked to have seen the bewildered expression on your face when you found your beautiful bird—caged for the night.

TONY: Look, Headmaster, this shock I was referring

to, it's made me think—well, I feel we shall have to face things as they are at very long last. Now I know this business has been a source of considerable interest and excitement to us all over a long period of years. It's kept us going, as you might say, when the results of the squash rackets competition and the state of the weather and the suspicion about who pinched the nail brush off the chain in the downstairs loo have been powerless to quicken the pulse. But it's gone too far, you know—we should never have started it.

ARTHUR: Of course you shouldn't. Now there's a twinge of conscience.

TONY: You know as much as I do. There's never been a breath of anything amiss.

ARTHUR (*singing bitterly*): "Tell me the old, old, story. . . ."

TONY: It started as an occupation. Like Halma or sardines. It's kept us from growing old.

ARTHUR: Bluff your way out of it, like when the waiter comes with the bill and " Most unfortunately my cheque book caught fire in my overcoat pocket."

TONY: Must we go on pretending? I don't even fancy Lily. Hardly my type.

ARTHUR (*aghast*): What are you saying?

TONY: That I don't love your wife. . . .

ARTHUR: You don't?

TONY: And never have.

ARTHUR (*with quiet fury*): You unspeakable hound. (*Beginning to shout.*) You don't love her? My God, I ought to strike you Peters.

TONY: That young Fay Knockbroker remains my ideal. Small and yellow and red hot. The girl you have to keep on protecting from the wicked results of her own innocence.

ARTHUR: But Bin. . . .

TONY: Not my sort at all. A very decent, under-standing sort, naturally: but the sort you'd always cram into the dicky if you had a girl like Fay to ride with in front.

ARTHUR: You don't love Bin?

TONY: I'm afraid not. . . .

ARTHUR: She's given you the best years of her life. . . .

TONY: Really Headmaster . . . I feel we ought to face these facts squarely . . . otherwise . . . well it may have, perhaps it's already had . . . results we didn't forsee.

ARTHUR: Bin. Poor girl. She mustn't ever guess.

TONY (*gently*): You are . . . fond of your wife, Headmaster?

ARTHUR: Fond of her. I *love* her, Peters. When I married I expected it would be for companionship—I'd known friendship before, Peters, genuine friendship. Someone to tramp around Wales with, to give a fill from your pouch, to share a hunk of cold Christmas pudding on a Boxing Day morning by Beachy Head—marriage is different, Peters. It takes place with a *woman*.

TONY: So I've been led to believe.

ARTHUR: And with a woman as attractive, soft, yielding, feminine as my Bin.

TONY: You take that view of her?

ARTHUR: Who mustn't ever be hurt . . . Oh it's hard. I tell you that at once, Peters, to live with such a feminine person as a woman in your life.

TONY: Problems arise of course.

ARTHUR: We had our work to do. We had the school to serve. Our lives aren't ours I told her. We're dedicated to the boys. And all the time all I wanted was to stay in bed with her all day only occasionally getting up for bread and marmalade.

TONY: Really. (*A long, embarrassed pause.*)

ARTHUR: Women are sensitive creatures, Peters. Lily mustn't be allowed to guess at what you've just told me.

TONY (*gestures resignedly*): But it's led to this. . . .

ARTHUR: She mustn't be *hurt*. Lily must never be *hurt*.

[*Pause.*]

TONY: You'll perhaps resent my saying this Arthur, and that's the risk I'm bound to take. But if you don't want Lily hurt . . . sometimes I'm bound to notice. . . .

ARTHUR (*proudly*): I shout at her you mean?

TONY: Well, not exactly coo.

ARTHUR: That's love. . . .

TONY: Oh yes?

ARTHUR: It takes people in different ways. Now when *you* want to make love to her I've noticed. . . .

TONY: But really.

ARTHUR: You make a joke. You pretend to be at the North Pole. You sing a song.

TONY: My weakness: I'm not serious.

ARTHUR: But when I see all that I love about my wife. The way she twists the hair over her ears when the time comes to make out a list. The soft smile she gives when no one's looking. How she shuts in laughter with the palm of her hand. . . . Then, I feel so small and angry. I see myself so powerless, so drawn into her that once I let myself go, all I believe in, all I'm dedicated to would be spent on afternoons of bread and marmalade. Then I shout. I don't know why it is. The terms of endearment I'm meaning to say just come out screaming. Is it a natural reaction?

TONY: I hardly know.

ARTHUR: And the agony of being in a room without her. The doubt and the anxiety that she'll be taken from me by the time I get back.

TONY: Really. We've got to stop it. This performance of ours has had its influence on Caroline. . . .

ARTHUR: Caroline? She's innocent of it all. She doesn't enter . . .

TONY: It has to stop, Headmaster.

ARTHUR: Who's going to stop it?

TONY: I am.

ARTHUR: You couldn't stop a catch.

TONY: I'm in duty bound. . . . (*Standing up.*)

ARTHUR: To tell Bin you don't love her. . . .

TONY: To tell the truth. For Caroline.

ARTHUR (*standing up, facing him*): Tony Peters. I need you. I know I have a sense of dedication which my wife doesn't altogether understand. In a way I'm a hard row for a woman like Bin to furrow. I shout. I'm a prey to irritation. I can't imitate snowstorms. I've forgotten all the jokes I've ever heard. She needs the bright lights, Peters, the music. The interest of another man. I knew that soon after I married her. I can't tell you how relieved I was the day you walked through those French windows. Then I knew my married life was safe at last.

TONY (*sitting down, bewildered*): Headmaster. This is a thought I would have put well beyond you.

ARTHUR (*solicitous*): I've shocked you?

TONY: Deeply. Deeply shocked.

ARTHUR: Together, all these years, we've kept Lily so happy.

TONY: You seem, Headmaster, to have the most tenuous grasp of morality.

ARTHUR: My temper and your songs—what a crowded, eventful time we've given her. And you must confess, Peters, it's been an interest for you. I mean there can't still be so many irons in your fire these days, whatever your part in Earls Court may have been.

TONY: Oh, Headmaster. I don't know what you're trying to find, but you're getting dangerously warm.

ARTHUR: We depend on each other, Peters. You mustn't tell her. We all depend on each other. . . .

TONY: But the younger generation? What are we doing for it?

ARTHUR: Our best, Peters. Let's allow ourselves that. . . .

TONY: But when I walked through these French windows. . . .

ARTHUR: You took on a job, Peters. You can't get out of it now.

TONY: I shouldn't have been singing. That was when I made my great mistake. . . .

[*The kitchen door opens. Lily enters smoking a cigarette, carrying a plate of bread and butter.*]

LILY: Has Caroline had her tea? I've been cutting all this bread and butter. The trouble with living here, the butter gets as hard as the rock of Gibraltar. It blasts great holes in your sliced bread.

TONY: Don't mention Gibraltar, Lily.

ARTHUR: There you go. Trying to pretend it's cold.

[*Lily drops cigarette ash on the bread, blows it off and sits down.*]

LILY: Out in the kitchen I heard men's voices rising and falling, rising and falling. What've you two been talking about now?

TONY: About you.

LILY: How nice.

ARTHUR: Tony's confessed.

LILY: Confessed?

ARTHUR: What he feels about you.

LILY: What he feels. (*She looks delightedly at Tony*). Have you Tony? (*She's biting bread and butter and smoking at the same time.*) What did you say?

ARTHUR: Do you want to tell my wife, Peters? Do you want to put a stop to this whole business, once and for all?

[*They both look at him. Tony gasps, smiles, and then gets up and walks up and down talking in clipped naval accents.*]

TONY: "Ladies and gentlemen. It is my duty to inform you that we have struck an iceberg. At nine-o-hundred hours, fish were noticed swimming in the first-class bath water. All ports have been alerted and in approximately ten-oo hours they will start looking for us by helicopter. If the ship has already sunk we will rendezvous at latitude 9.700 and bob about in the water together as long as possible. . . ."

[*He comes to rest behind Lily's chair.*]

Oh Lily. I can't tell you how complicated it's all become.

ARTHUR: No. You can't.

[*Caroline enters from the boys' side, left. She is carrying her suitcase which she puts down on the floor.*]

LILY: Caroline!

[*Caroline unhooks her mackintosh from the back of the door and slowly puts it on. Arthur and Lily watch her fearfully. She picks up the suitcase and stands in front of the French windows.*]

ARTHUR: She's going for a walk.
LILY: Probably that's it.
TONY: Haven't you noticed the suitcase? Does she usually go for a walk with a suitcase?
LILY: Caroline. Put it down.

[*She gets up and goes towards Caroline. Tony puts out his arm and stops her.*]

TONY: Better to let her do what she wants.
LILY: What does she want? How can she tell us?

[*Caroline opens her mouth. Long silence in which she is making an enormous effort until she says—*)

CAROLINE: I want to go to London.

[*They look at her in amazement. In dead silence Caroline puts down her suitcase.*]

I've got a job with the Threadneedle Street Branch of the Chesterfield and National Bank. I start at a salary of seven pounds ten shillings a week.

[*She takes the letter and hands it to Lily. Lily crying, looks at it and hands it to Arthur. Arthur reads it and gives it to Tony.*]

TONY: There seems to be some truth in what she says.
LILY: Stop her. Stop her leaving us, Arthur.
ARTHUR: She spoke. Our daughter spoke.

[*Tony gives Caroline back the letter.*]

CAROLINE: I have a third floor room at 109 Great Bidford Street which costs four pounds ten shillings a week, with board. I shall therefore have three pounds fifteen shillings a week left over. . . .

TONY: Caroline . . . I hate to disillusion you.

ARTHUR: She's talking. She's talking to me.

CAROLINE: Goodbye. (*She shakes Arthur's hand.*)

ARTHUR: Forgive me.

CAROLINE: Goodbye. (*She shakes Lily's hand.*)

LILY: What have we done wrong?

CAROLINE: Good-bye. (*She shakes Tony's hand.*)

TONY: Good-bye.

LILY: It's too late to go now. . . .

CAROLINE: The train leaves at 7.15 from Coldsands Station. Platform One. Change at Norwich. (*She goes out and closes the French windows. For a moment she stands looking in at them through the glass. Then she disappears.*)

TONY: Let's hope she's right about that.

LILY: Why didn't you stop her?

ARTHUR (*sitting down*): She spoke to me. She said good-bye.

TONY: Well, that's right, she did.

LILY (*standing distractedly in the middle of the room*): What shall I do?

TONY: Clear away the tea.

ARTHUR: Lily. There's something you ought to know about Caroline. She hasn't said anything for a long time.

[*Silence. Then Tony says:*]

TONY: We'd noticed that.

ARTHUR: You didn't comment?

[*Tony shrugs his shoulders.*]

ARTHUR: You didn't like to?

TONY: It seemed unnecessary.

ARTHUR: Kindness held you back?

LILY: We must stop her going.

TONY: She won't meet any harm.

ARTHUR: But you don't know why she didn't speak? I told you, Peters, all the terms of endearment start shouting and screaming when I utter them. When I love someone all my love turns to irritation. I lost my temper with Caroline! I hit her! I actually hit her!

LILY (*crossing towards him*): No dear. You didn't.

ARTHUR: How do you know?

TONY: We were here in the room. You didn't hit her, Headmaster.

ARTHUR (*deflated*): I did. I wanted to hit her. After that, I thought she didn't speak. The nervous shock. Was it the nervous shock do you think, either of you?

LILY: Perhaps she didn't want to.

TONY: Or she had nothing to say to us. Although we had enough to say to her. . . .

LILY: Who shall we talk to now?

TONY: Each other, Lily. Always to each other.

LILY: Caroline! Why should she have to go, Tony?

TONY: She has to go sometime.

ARTHUR: I made her go. I hit her. I must have hit her. There's no other explanation.

TONY (*sits down in the basket-chair and picks up his ukulele*): How shall we ever know?

ARTHUR: What do you mean. For God's sake explain what you mean?

TONY: Was it your temper or her temper that

stopped her speaking? Was it just the complete lack of interest that overcomes all children at the thought of the parents who gave them birth?

ARTHUR: I wasn't responsible?

TONY: What's responsible for Caroline as she is? What you told her? What you didn't tell her? The fact we told her a lie? The fact we told her the truth? Look back, Arthur. Look back, Lily do. What made us what we are? Anything our fathers and mothers said? More likely something that happened when we were all alone. Something we thought of for ourselves, looking for a passable disguise in a dusty attic, or for a path that didn't exist in the hot summer in the middle of a wood that smelt of nettles.

ARTHUR: Is that how you found things out?

TONY: My dear old headmaster. I've never found out anything. I'm not a parent, but in my weak moments, like this afternoon, I've wanted to tell things to the young. Why do we do it? Not to give them information, but to make them repeat our lives. That's all. It's finished with us and we don't want it to be finished. We'd like them to do it for us—all over again. It'll be better for Caroline to work in the bank. If only her *adding* weren't quite so shaky. Let's hope she errs, Headmaster, on the side of generosity.

[*Lily gets up and begins to put things on a tray.*]

ARTHUR: What are you doing, Bin?

LILY: Clearing away the tea. (*She goes out with the tray.*)

TONY (*looking at his watch*): Just ten minutes and the boys have to stop their so called " free time " and be hoarded into prep. I shall sit with them in silence.

I'm not tempted to communicate with them any more.

ARTHUR: I'd better start to get the history corrected. Then I must take the roll-call. Let's hope the boys are all . . . still with us.

[*He goes over to the roll top desk. Starts marking exercise books.*]

TONY (*singing softly*):
   "Here we sit like birds in the wilderness,
      Birds in the wilderness.
      Birds in the wilderness.
   Here we sit like birds in the wilderness . . ."

ARTHUR: Peters.

TONY (*singing*): "Down in Demerara. . . ."

ARTHUR: Was Henry the Third the *son* of Henry the Second?

TONY: He certainly wasn't his daughter.

ARTHUR: It doesn't *look* right somehow.

TONY: I suspect him of having been the son of King John.

ARTHUR: This boy misled me.

TONY: You can't rely on *them*. Not for accurate information.

ARTHUR: Peters.

TONY: Yes, Headmaster.

ARTHUR: Bin hasn't taken it too well, Caroline going off like that.

TONY: A loss for us all, of course.

ARTHUR: It's taken a great deal from her.

TONY: Yes.

ARTHUR: It's more important than ever. . . .

TONY: What is?

ARTHUR: That we should keep going. Like we always have. If we stopped quarrelling over her now. . . .

TONY: Yes Headmaster?

ARTHUR: Think how empty her poor life would be.

TONY: And our lives?

ARTHUR: Empty too, perhaps.

TONY: You know, it must be almost twenty years ago that I came in through that window and made a joke. And now, it seems, I've got to live on that joke for ever.

[*Lily comes in. She shivers, rubs her hands and crouches by the electric fire to warm them.*]

LILY: It's cold.

ARTHUR: Nonsense.

LILY: It seems strange. Just the three of us. Shall we always be alone now?

ARTHUR: There it is.

TONY: You never know. Just when you felt most lonely in Earls Court I always noticed this, it was always the time when you met a bit of new. I remember feeling damned lonely one spring evening, about this time, walking down the Earls Court Road, and there was this beautiful girl, about eighteen, no older than Caroline in fact, her gloved finger pressed to a bell.

ARTHUR: I hope there's nothing disgusting about this reminisence Peters.

TONY: So I said nothing. I went and stood beside her. She gave me a glance. It wasn't exactly marching orders. Then the door was opened by another girl, slightly older. "Come in darling," she said. "I'm so glad you could bring your husband." So we sat us down to four courses and later as it came on to fog, it was carte blanche of the spare bedroom for the night. You see the hostess, it all turned out, had never seen the husband.

LILY: And that poor husband?

TONY: Unexpectedly lamed that very afternoon. A taxi had run over his foot, so she explained it in the spare room.

LILY: And you walked straight up to her?

TONY: Quick work wasn't it?

LILY: A quick worker, Tony.

TONY: No grass grows under Tony Peters, thank God.

ARTHUR: I made sure that story would end up as disgusting.

LILY: Oh Tony! What adventures you've had!

TONY: Adventures, thank goodness, still come to me.

[*He looks longingly at Lily. She puts an elbow on his knee and gazes into the electric fire.*]

ARTHUR: Isn't the room big enough? Do you have to sit on top of one another?

TONY: Now Headmaster. It'll soon be time for roll-call.

LILY (*thoughtfully*): I haven't really had many adventures. Have you, Arthur?

ARTHUR: What?

LILY: Had many adventures?

ARTHUR (*reading*): Was that Henry II?

TONY: Was what Henry II?

ARTHUR: The chap whose son was drowned?

TONY: Drowned?

ARTHUR: In the White Ship.

[*Tony picks up his ukulele and sings to Lily.*]

TONY (*singing*):
    "Here we sit like birds in the wilderness,
        Birds in the wilderness."

ARTHUR (*closing the exercise book and beginning to shout*): Peters. Bin. Stop goading me both of you. Don't you even wait now until I'm decently out of the room?

TONY (*singing*):
"Here we sit like birds in the wilderness,
    Down in Demerara."
                As the ship went down."

ARTHUR: (*standing up and hitting his desk with a tremendous crash with his fist*): Stop singing to my wife! Take your greedy eyes off her!

[*Arthur and Lily look at each other with deep affection. Tony plays a note on his ukulele. Arthur exits.*)

Curtain

I SPY

First produced by the B.B.C. Third Programme on 19th November, 1957. The cast was as follows:

MR. FRUTE	*Ralph Michael*
MRS. MORGAN	*Brenda Bruce*
GLADYS	*Marjorie Westbury*
LAWYER	*Gerald Cross*
CAPTAIN MORGAN	*Michael Shepley*

Produced by Nesta Pain

Produced on B.B.C. Television on 28th January, 1958 when the cast was as follows:

MR. FRUTE	*Donald Pleasence*
MRS. MORGAN	*Brenda Bruce*
GLADYS	*Vi Stevens*
LAWYER	*Gerald Cross*
CAPTAIN MORGAN	*William Fox*

Produced by Douglas Allen

The stage is divided into three acting areas. Back stage, against a clear background, a row of railings and a shelter represent the promenade of the seaside town, Cold Sands. On the left of the stage a serving table, a screen and one laid restaurant table, together with a sign on which a lugubrious-looking stag is painted, represent the serving room and part of the dining room of the " Stag at Bay " hotel. Stage right a desk, a telephone and two chairs represent the lawyer's office.

The three areas are not lit at the same time. The action is divided between them.

As the curtain rises the back area is faintly lit. Somewhere a barrel organ is playing " Home Sweet Home ".

The lights fade on the background and the hotel side of the stage is lit to discover Frute, a small, unhappy, middle aged man, dressed as a waiter, standing with four soup plates precariously balanced up one arm. Mrs. Morgan, a pleasant-looking woman in her thirties, is watching him anxiously.

The plates crash to the ground. Mrs. Morgan stoops to pick up the pieces. Frute looks ruefully down at the wreckage.

FRUTE: Careless again!

MRS. MORGAN: Let me help.

FRUTE (*too discouraged to help her*): I feel I shall never master it. . . .

MRS. MORGAN: What, Mr. Frute?

FRUTE: The trick waiters are supposed to have. When four plates lie up that arm and another spins in the hand like Chinese juggling.

MRS. MORGAN: Come now, Mr. Frute, it's not so hard. When you've been a waiter so long. . . .

FRUTE: Not so long as you may think, Mrs. Morgan. You, you're so skilful. Have you been, many years, a waitress?

MRS. MORGAN: Fifteen. I think it makes fifteen.

FRUTE: A good stint.

MRS. MORGAN: The feet suffer.

FRUTE: They do. That's just it. I long for a sit down.

MRS. MORGAN: Isn't the dining room empty by now?

FRUTE: Almost.

MRS. MORGAN: Let's have a look see. (*She peers into the darkness on the other side of the screen.*) The honeymooners have just come in. They've been on the prom and they're *soaking*!

FRUTE: I don't feel up to the honeymooners tonight. Shall I . . .?

MRS. MORGAN: Yes?

FRUTE: Shall I tell them it's all off, except the cold?

MRS. MORGAN: You could. But would it be kind? They're in love.

FRUTE: Oblivious, might we hope, to what they're tasting?

MRS. MORGAN: We only honeymoon it once, Mr. Frute.

FRUTE: Well, some of us.

MRS. MORGAN: And in love, I feel sure, they'd fancy something hot.

FRUTE: I must soldier on?

MRS. MORGAN: No, you have a little rest. I'll get the order.

[*Mrs. Morgan exits. Frute, sitting on the serving table, brings out a note book and pencil and begins, laboriously, to write. Mrs. Morgan comes bustling back.*]

That's alright, dear. They've ordered.

[*Mrs. Morgan shouts to an unseen cook off stage. Frute is still making notes.*]

MRS. MORGAN: Gladys!
GLADYS (*off*): Aw Ug Ug Ug.
MRS. MORGAN: Two brown windsors. Two steak pies. Cabbage and chips.
GLADYS (*off*): 'Ips off.
MRS. MORGAN: Make it boiled then, dear. There now, something nice and hot for them.

[*She turns round and sees Frute taking notes.*]

You been writing again, Mr. Frute?
FRUTE (*embarrassed, he shuts his notebook*): Just . . . something to write up.
MRS. MORGAN: You do write a lot, don't you? Big family to keep up with, I expect.
FRUTE: No family at all, Mrs. Morgan.
MRS. MORGAN: Business, then?
FRUTE: Purely business.
GLADYS (*off*): Two ownzizzors.
MRS. MORGAN: Gladys *is* slippy tonight. Mind the lift, dear.

[*Crash of lift, off stage. Mrs. Morgan exits. Returns with two plates of soup.*]

There, she always gets the rims all sloshy. . . .
FRUTE: Shall I take it?

MRS. MORGAN: No, you sit and rest. Give you a chance to finish up your writing. Besides, the windsor stains so if you do have a spill.

[*Mrs. Morgan disappears into the darkness on the other side of the screen. While she is gone, Frute writes again. He is swearing at a broken pencil as she returns.*]

FRUTE: Damn.

MRS. MORGAN: Something happened?

FRUTE: I've broken my pencil, the one and only.

MRS. MORGAN: Here, borrow my indelible.

FRUTE: That's kind.

MRS. MORGAN: Don't suck it, now. I often do that when the figures baffle. Then a tea or a hot dinner will stare up, and me not realising I'm frothing all purple at the mouth, epileptic. . . .

[*He goes on writing as she says:*]

Really, those honeymooners. He wants wine.

FRUTE (*looking up*): Wine, Mrs. Morgan?

MRS. MORGAN: I told him we only had the Graves or the Bones—

FRUTE: What's he want with wine?

MRS. MORGAN: To add a bit of colour to life, perhaps.

FRUTE: If you try to add colour to life it only ends, in my business experience, in the payment of high legal costs.

MRS. MORGAN: Better humour him. I'll get it.

[*Mrs. Morgan exits. Frute begins to speak as he laboriously writes. He uses the more stilted, classier voice in which, as a private detective, he gives evidence in court.*]

FRUTE (*confidentially*): In re Captain Morgan's divorce:

your observer Frute takes the liberty to report. It was no doubt fortunate from the point of view of keeping a close watch on Mrs. Morgan, that your observer was able to obtain the post of temporary waiter at the "Stag at Bay" Hotel, Cold Sands. However, your observer is not finding the art of waiting even in a temporary capacity, an altogether easy one to master. Neither is it always convenient to combine prompt attention in the dining-room with the many and intricate duties expected of a skilled Private Detective. . . .

[*Frute hears something. Then tiptoes off, writing, to investigate. Fade out light on serving room.*]

[*The lawyer's office is illuminated. The lawyer and the Captain have entered and taken their seats at the desk during Frute's last speech.*]

[*The lawyer is reading from Frute's report.*]

LAWYER: "Be that as it may, your observer has at present formed the opinion that Mrs. Morgan is leading a life of so-called innocence." (*He puts down the report.*) Well, Captain Morgan. That's Frute's first report on your wife. Nothing sensational as yet, but useful spadework, do admit. Very useful spadework.

CAPT. MORGAN: It's pretty distasteful.

LAWYER: Of course.

CAPT. MORGAN: When I married I only asked for a little love, a touch of infatuation. I was young. You may find it hard to credit.

LAWYER: On the contrary, Captain Morgan. I assume you to have been quite young, in your time.

CAPT. MORGAN: It was natural to expect her to be

devoted. A normal woman would have been blindly devoted. I gave her the earth.

LAWYER (*turning over a file*): Yours is a very slim file for a matrimonial, but let that pass. No years of nagging, no decades of sullen silence here. Three hundred and forty-two, no a miscast, three hundred and forty-one, if my mathematics serve me, days, and naturally, it must follow, nights, of married life. Then your wife demands a separation. You didn't argue?

CAPT. MORGAN: One has a certain pride.

LAWYER: Understood. So you signed the Separation Agreement for—was it five shillings a week?

CAPT. MORGAN: Seven and six.

LAWYER: Indeed! But it's not paid as she . . . vanishes. Then, from a clear sky, we get the post-card of last March. Postmark Cold Sands. Simply states, your wife's hand is childishly legible, "Hope you are well, Edna". We set our man Frute on to her and she's gone to ground as a waitress at the Stag at Bay Hotel. Now, you're anxious to shed her without delay?

CAPT. MORGAN: No desperate hurry.

LAWYER: To my other clients marriage is the great, heavy eiderdown to be kicked off in the hot middle of the night.

CAPT. MORGAN: If she could have been made to see it straight, she'd have loved me.

LAWYER (*reassuringly*): Not a doubt.

CAPT. MORGAN: Her mother should have *spoken* to her.

LAWYER: Parents are so silent.

CAPT. MORGAN: What could have been *wrong* with me?

LAWYER: Nothing, I feel sure.

CAPT. MORGAN: I gave her everything.

LAWYER: Indeed, yes.

CAPT. MORGAN (*a burst of confidence*): One doesn't boast about the commissioned rank, but I'd lived a pretty clean life. Doctor checked me when I had marriage in view. That was only fair. Saturdays with the Richmond Cross Country Run was a habit of mine. As far as fitness went I was top-notch by the wedding breakfast. There was money in the bank, a house on mortgage and a serviceable roadster. Was there anything a normal woman wouldn't have loved?

LAWYER: I can think of nothing at the moment.

CAPT. MORGAN: And when I picked her out....

LAWYER: Let me see, before she married you she was.....

CAPT. MORGAN: It's pretty sordid.

LAWYER: Her job of work?

CAPT. MORGAN: No, I mean the divorce. A private detective. The Law Court crammed with doubtful women in black dresses and men with co-respondent's shoes. The headlines, "*Captain's wife antics in seaside hotel*". I may have been a bit of a romantic in my younger days. Running along Richmond Park, chasing the little, bright scraps of paper, my thoughts often turned to love and marriage. I got a different picture, then, of how it was all going to be.

LAWYER: Be of good heart, Captain Morgan. The divorce will be quite simple. All we need is a touch of evidence. Has love, for instance, beckoned to Mrs. Morgan? I mean since she parted from your good self.

CAPT. MORGAN: Love? With her it doesn't enter in.

LAWYER: After all, she's a woman. We can count on the frailty of her sex, ably assisted by the tireless Frute. If she is addicted to love, Frute will unearth it.

CAPT. MORGAN: More than I could. Good luck to him.

LAWYER: Good luck to him, Captain Morgan? Good luck to us all. I'll see you out.

[*The lawyer ushers the Captain out of his office. Fade out light on office.*]

[*Fade in light on serving room. Frute enters. He is holding a vegetable dish and two spoons in one hand. He makes a scoop at the dish and drops the spoons.*]

MRS. MORGAN (*off*): Mr. Frute. What are you doing?

FRUTE: Trying out your expert way of serving the cabbage.

[*Mrs. Morgan enters and picks up the spoons and puts the dish on the table.*]

MRS. MORGAN: Don't embark on it, Mr. Frute, until I've had the chance of giving you a few lessons.

FRUTE: Mrs. Morgan. . . .

MRS. MORGAN: Yes?

FRUTE: Am I right in thinking that you're "off" this afternoon?

MRS. MORGAN: Well, I am.

FRUTE: And doing—anything in particular?

MRS. MORGAN (*pause—pleased*): Not really.

FRUTE: Meeting perhaps Mister Special?

MRS. MORGAN: No one special.

FRUTE: I see. . . .

MRS. MORGAN: As a matter of fact, Mr. Frute, I'll tell you quite candidly, I've been living alone so long. . . .

FRUTE: Yes. . . .

MRS. MORGAN: And it's on the days off one feels it most.

FRUTE: Like me, you haven't picked up many friends?

MRS. MORGAN: When you're working you forget about it, but in the time off, it hits you. Eating alone in cafes.

FRUTE: Sitting alone in the cinema, reading the newspaper when they turn up the lights for organ music. . . .

MRS. MORGAN: No call to put on a best dress and no helpful hand behind you to zip you in. . . .

FRUTE: And this afternoon?

MRS. MORGAN: If nothing transpires I may go out with Gladys. She's a good sort, really, when you get her on your own level. Not shouting up that lift. . . .

FRUTE: If you're really fixed up with Gladys. . . .

MRS. MORGAN: We've nothing firm.

FRUTE: You may . . . meet someone else?

MRS. MORGAN: I mean if you, Mr. Frute. . . .

FRUTE: Oh Mrs. Morgan. I'm afraid that would not be possible.

MRS. MORGAN: You're busy?

FRUTE: It wouldn't be (*grandly*) professional etiquette.

MRS. MORGAN (*mystified*): I suppose not. . . . Well, I'll be seeing you.

FRUTE: I don't think so. But I, Mrs. Morgan, shall be seeing you. Oh, Mrs. Morgan. . . .

MRS. MORGAN: Yes?

FRUTE: Before you go?

MRS. MORGAN (*hopefully*): Yes, Mr. Frute?

FRUTE: Might I ask. . . .

MRS. MORGAN: Of course.

FRUTE: For the further loan of the pencil.

MRS. MORGAN (*disappointed*): Well, here it is.

[*She goes, and Frute begins to write. As he writes he speaks.*]

FRUTE: Mrs. Morgan is about to embark on her period of "Time Off". This is the period when she is most likely to indulge in marital infidelity if she be so minded. Your observer Frute proposes to keep in constant, but discreet attendance. . . .

[*Frute gets his hat and exits after Mrs. Morgan. Mrs. Morgan and Gladys appear backstage by the railings and the shelter. Frute enters and speaks confidentially to the audience.*]

FRUTE : . . . Mrs. Morgan appears to be spending the time off with Gladys from the kitchen. This is a strange choice having regard to the fact that Mrs. Morgan is such a handsome, indeed an attractive individual.

[*Mrs. Morgan and Gladys turn up the collars of their mackintoshes as they walk.*]

Weather conditions for keeping observation are not ideal. There is a distinct fog from the North Sea. Winters at Cold Sands are said to be severe. They could hardly be more severe than the summers. . . . However, you may rest assured that climatic conditions will in no way deter your observer Frute. . . .

[*They are by the shelter.*]

MRS. MORGAN: It's coming down torrential again. Slip into the shelter, shall we?
GLADYS: Mmmmmm.

[*They sit in the shelter. Frute crosses furtively and sits on a seat behind them. He peers at them and writes.*]

MRS. MORGAN: It's not often you get drawn to another human being, is it, Gladys? But this Mr. Frute is so nicely spoken, and a child when it comes to plates. . . .

GLADYS: Yerrum.

MRS. MORGAN: And he's got such a sensitive look. I never remember such a fine-drawn appearance on any man. But when I was quite young we took in a lodger, ever such a gentle, sensitive type of man, and once I burst into his bedroom unbeknownst and he was saying his prayers. He really was. Kneeling by his bed, and I saw that hole shining pink in the sole of his sock and I thought poor fellow, and I felt so sorry for him, as when this Mr. Frute breaks a plate. . . .

GLADYS: Deeyerrr.

MRS. MORGAN: Well, I was telling you about this fellow with the hole in his sock. So fine-drawn he was, and one day the police came for him and they removed him from us and it seemed that he had not two wives but five, and very nice types of women and all in different parts of England, the Channel Islands and the Isle of Man. Not that our waiter, of course. . . . Sometimes I wonder if he *is* a waiter. What if he were doing it all for some *woman*. . . . But that's nonsense like you read in those weekly books. . . .

GLADYS: Nummmmm.

MRS. MORGAN: No offence, Gladys dear, but you're not a great one for conversation, are you?

FRUTE (*speaking as he writes*): Your observer can only describe this as a summer blizzard. (*Sneezes.*) There are distinct traces of hail. (*He peers out to sea.*) There seems to be some distress at sea. The Cold Sands lifeboat is apparently being launched. From the few sentences which I could hear, it seemed that

Mrs. Morgan was discussing some man for whom she felt a decided glow of affection. In the roar of the summer blizzard your observer was unable to hear the name of the said individual. . . .

MRS. MORGAN: Come on then, Gladys. We'll miss the picture. . . .

[*They get up and we see them walk down to the railings to exit. Frute exits, following them. Slowly all the lights fade. When they come on again Frute is sitting in the serving room writing.*]

FRUTE (*speaking as he writes*): Without any opportunity to change into dry clothing, your observer followed Mrs. Morgan to the Pix Picture Palace in High Street where a lengthy "Double Feature" programme was viewed. Halfway through the Newsreel, Mrs. Morgan was addressed by a strange man in the two-and-three's. Mrs. Morgan at once, with some delicacy and financial sacrifice, changed her seat and that of Gladys to the one-and-nines. Your observer is not of the opinion that this man was in any way connected with the individual of whom Mrs. Morgan had spoken with warmth and affection. (*Cough.*) Your observer intends, with redoubled vigilance, to keep watch on all of Mrs. Morgan's activities. (*Burst of coughs and sneezes.*) Despite his, at present, extremely heavy cold. . . .

[*Fade out light on serving room. Frute exits. Fade in on lawyer's office. The lawyer and Captain enter and take their seats.*]

LAWYER: It appears our observer has a heavy cold.
CAPT. MORGAN (*anxious*): He won t crock up?

LAWYER: Frute will soldier on. He is a little terrier after an affair of the heart. And doesn't it seem we've struck oil?

CAPT. MORGAN: Oil?

LAWYER: Talking, you see, of another man.

CAPT. MORGAN (*pause, then very excited*): Of course. There must be another man. He's the answer to the problem that's tortured me all these years.

LAWYER: This. . . .

CAPT. MORGAN: Enticer. This C.3. rat. This thin, brown foreigner with his big car and his Golders Green Wholesale Grocery and his long black oily sideboards. . . .

LAWYER: Furniture?

CAPT. MORGAN: Hair.

LAWYER: You know him?

CAPT. MORGAN: Of course not.

LAWYER: But?

CAPT. MORGAN: He's the missing link. She loved me. But he mesmerised her. Now, poor girl, she wants to come creeping back.

LAWYER: You'd have her?

CAPT. MORGAN: No. Pride.

LAWYER: Ah!

CAPT. MORGAN: Of course he's got the power of his bank balance. Even though he's bald and fat and red-eyed and calls his sitting-room the lounge.

LAWYER: But I thought you described. . . .

CAPT. MORGAN: We don't know him exactly yet. We only know he *must* exist.

LAWYER: Can we go quite so far? The report merely says that a man was mentioned.

CAPT. MORGAN: But she left me. Any Court would draw the inference.

LAWYER: I fear not. After all, it may have been an innocent. . . .

CAPT. MORGAN: Innocent! You're a lawyer, you don't believe that?

LAWYER: My dear Captain, as a lawyer I believe nothing. My mind is a lean, well-dieted stomach, only capable of taking in that which can satisfy it beyond reasonable doubt. And yet I know that out of the ten persons with whom I travel daily in the train, one must be an adulterer, another a bigamist, a third a slanderer of goods and so on. If it were not so, these offences, in all their legal profusion, would not exist. I see no reason why your wife should be different from the rest of humanity. But at present, I fear, I smell no odour of proof.

CAPT. MORGAN: It'll come. If Frute only sticks to her.

LAWYER: He'll stick to her, Captain Morgan. Like a leech. . . .

[*Fade out light on lawyer's office as lawyer exits, showing the Captain to the door.*]

[*Fade in light on serving room. Frute is trying to speak to Gladys. Obviously he is having no success and she exits. He sits down to write, speaking as he does so.*]

FRUTE: In the days that have passed since Mrs. Morgan's 'time off' there has been no further sign of the individual of whom she was heard to confide. Your observer has attempted to elicit the name of this individual from the female Gladys, but the said Gladys is of the 'strong and silent' variety, and your observer was reluctant to let the 'cat out of the bag' by pressing his enquiries 'home'.

[*Frute has a fit of coughing as Mrs. Morgan enters. He puts his notebook away guiltily.*]

MRS. MORGAN: The trouble is you're not really fit for work with that terrible cold on you. We saw you the other night, Gladys and I.

FRUTE (*sneeze*): Did you, Mrs. Morgan?

MRS. MORGAN: We saw you in the cinema. We waved, but you didn't pay all that attention. You looked a bit miserable as I remarked to Gladys, as if you were in your wet clothes.

FRUTE: Mrs. Morgan, to be frank with you, so I was.

MRS. MORGAN: Enjoy your 'time off' did you?

FRUTE: Not specially.

MRS. MORGAN: On the front were you?

FRUTE: Yes. Did you see the wreck?

MRS. MORGAN: What wreck?

FRUTE: They launched the lifeboat.

MRS. MORGAN: Bless you, that wasn't the lifeboat!

FRUTE: Those grim-faced men in oil skins?

MRS. MORGAN: Holiday-makers. That was the pleasure trip, from the end of the pier. And you thought there'd been a catastrophe. . . . (*Laughs.*)

FRUTE (*laughing with her*): A sinking at the least.

MRS. MORGAN (*laughing*): And suppose if you'd dived in to save a life.

FRUTE (*laughing, then serious*): Well, hardly Mrs. Morgan, I breast stroke it a few yards. Not exactly up to Cross Channel standard.

MRS. MORGAN (*very serious*): But I'm sure you'd have had a try, if anyone was in distress.

FRUTE (*flattered*): Well, a stab at it perhaps.

MRS. MORGAN: There now, you see.

[*Pause.*]

FRUTE: Mrs. Morgan, since I have been working here I will say you've shown me every kindness. I regard you, if I may say so, without offence, as a sincerely helpful type of individual. . . .

MRS. MORGAN: Go along. . . .

FRUTE: Always ready, as you've shown many a time when a plate slipped or I got the Golden Roll in ahead of the Brown Windsor, to rescue a fellow being.

MRS. MORGAN: What about you, Mr. Frute? The way you stood poised on that pier, ready to dive off when you thought there'd been a wrecking. . . .

FRUTE: Not quite poised perhaps. But to return to you. . . .

MRS. MORGAN: Soaked to the skin. Scanning that sea for survivors. . . .

FRUTE: What I'm leading to, Mrs. Morgan, is that, only you can help one if it isn't a liberty.

MRS. MORGAN: Anything, Mr. Frute.

FRUTE: It's a business matter. It's not going too smoothly as it so happens. . . .

MRS. MORGAN: I'm sorry. . . .

FRUTE: I don't like to approach you directly like this.

MRS. MORGAN: Whatever can it be?

FRUTE: Well then, not to make a meal, rumour has it. . . .

MRS. MORGAN: Rumour?

FRUTE: That there may be a gentleman in whom you are especially interested.

MRS. MORGAN: Don't be so silly, Mr. Frute. There's only ever been one man in my life, and just my luck we didn't hit it.

FRUTE: The Captain?

MRS. MORGAN: How did you know?

FRUTE: Rumour.

MRS. MORGAN: Has it, I suppose.

FRUTE: Exactly, yes. You didn't hit it apparently.

MRS. MORGAN: We met in the early war years.

" Marry me," he said, " I shall soon be sent abroad and killed."

FRUTE: Sound reason.

MRS. MORGAN: It didn't work out like that. They put him in charge of an Army Post Office at Pullborough. He got a sleeping-out pass every night.

FRUTE: What led you two to matrimony?

MRS. MORGAN: Loneliness perhaps. My mother and father had passed. I was working in the West End of London.

FRUTE: Shop assistant?

MRS. MORGAN: Cigarette kiosk on Platform 9 at Paddington. The Captain made the journey regular. I knew nothing about him really, and of me he only knew what he saw.

FRUTE: Which was. . . .

MRS. MORGAN: The head and shoulders. A kiosk doesn't give all that away. Afterwards he blamed that kiosk, and as he used to say, it was the mix up of social classes due to the war that led him on to marry me—

FRUTE: Socially conscious?

MRS. MORGAN: That I didn't resent, but such a jumpy nervous type of man. Thank God, he'd say, I'll always keep one bullet in this revolver for you. . . .

FRUTE: Why on earth?

MRS. MORGAN: In case the war picture changed, and I got raped by the Russians. . . . I couldn't see it his way. Let's meet that little trouble, I told him often enough, when it comes. Then he got so overexcited. He took it in his head that I'd only married him for his little black saloon car. We hadn't any petrol for it anyway. So he gave that little car to a brother officer. Then he said that I'd only married him because of the handsome gold watch I'd spotted on his wrist. So he smashed that with a heavy hammer and shouted out " Now love me for myself alone." Or he'd run out of the bathroom, even his dark horn rims left off. " This is the man " he'd cry out, " stripped of his regimentals—can't you love me for what I am?" Put like that, Mr. Frute, and I just couldn't. I told him so, so he gave me the Separation Agreement. " A gentleman can't turn you off with nothing," he said, as he signed for that seven and six a week. Never kept it up, of course.

FRUTE: Ungenerous?

MRS. MORGAN: Always suspicious—always wanting to be loved. And always taking little lumps of coal off the fire because he said I'd only married him for the extra fuel allotment. One year's married life and I've never been so cold. Then he'd shout, " I'm extremely popular, I'm well liked at Pullborough. Why can't you be the same as everyone else? Love me, damn you." Well, I didn't and that was that. It wasn't a home like I remembered.

FRUTE: Which was that?

MRS. MORGAN: Dalston Junction. My father's place.

FRUTE: They can be comfortable round there.

MRS. MORGAN: Small and compact. Nothing big about it.

FRUTE: But. . . .

MRS. MORGAN: Warm. You'd come back from school or shopping with a wind cutting your face and your fingers stiff as chicken claws, and to open that door—it was like a kiss of air from the underground.

FRUTE: That. . . .

MRS. MORGAN: Was what I appreciated. A welcome to unfreeze your face. Father, he'd come home every Friday and out he'd spread his whole wage packet on the oil-cloth. He didn't ask to be loved just for himself. A different class of man entirely.

FRUTE: So you left . . . the Captain?

MRS. MORGAN: I didn't think he ever saw the point.

FRUTE: And since that day. There's been no one?

MRS. MORGAN: If I'd met a man who didn't expect anyone to like him. . . .

FRUTE: You never have?

MRS. MORGAN: No. And *your* home?

FRUTE: Run by the Essex County Council. Between eight and nine hundred of us. A big family like that, the superintendent always explained, rubs the edges off you.

MRS. MORGAN: I'm sorry. But matrimony has never—appealed?

FRUTE: Never come my way, in *private* life, that is. Too late now, we really must assume.

MRS. MORGAN: Well, Mr. Frute.

FRUTE: Yes, Mrs. Morgan?

MRS. MORGAN: We seem to be two of a kind.

[*Pause.*]

Another lunch time.

FRUTE (*slapping his pocket*): I'm clean out of smokes.

MRS. MORGAN: Slip out for a few if you'd care to. I'll polish these up.

FRUTE: I'm leaving all the work to you. . . .

MRS. MORGAN: Go on. Do you good to get a breath of air that didn't smell of soup.

FRUTE: I won't be many minutes. . . . (*He goes out.*)

[*Mrs. Morgan breathes on a glass, sings and polishes.*]

MRS. MORGAN (*singing*):
> " Mid pleasures and palaces
> Long may we roam.
> We always come back for . . .
> There's no place like home."

[*She exits singing.*]

[*Fade in back stage.*]

[*A man is sitting reading a newspaper in the shelter. He lowers his newspaper as Frute enters and passes him. He is revealed as Captain Morgan.*]

CAPT. MORGAN: Here. What's your name? Frute?

[*Frute stops, bewildered.*]

FRUTE: Whoever. . . .
CAPT. MORGAN: I'm Captain Morgan.
FRUTE: Really, this is very distressing. . . .
CAPT. MORGAN: For *you*?
FRUTE: It's not etiquette. A direct approach from the client. It's not professional. A gentleman never bandies words with his detective. A gentleman speaks to his solicitor who speaks to me, his detective, upon the telephone. Oh dear, this is very unknown.
CAPT. MORGAN: It's hardly pleasant for me. I need your reassurance.
FRUTE: You need . . .?
CAPT. MORGAN: Look here. When I spotted you I assumed you were following my wife.
FRUTE: No. As a matter of fact. . . .
CAPT. MORGAN: What?
FRUTE (*lamely*): Just slipped out for a packet of smokes.
CAPT. MORGAN: Really?
FRUTE: Now, don't worry. At the moment she's laying up the lunch and I'm on my way back to . . . help her. She can't escape.
CAPT. MORGAN: And the other scoundrel. You have a finger on him?

FRUTE: Who?

CAPT. MORGAN: The frightful R.A.F. salesman outsider with his spotted scarf and his walrus whiskers and his, " Down the hatch, here's to the Good Old Duke " in the saloon bar until half an hour past closing time. . . .

FRUTE: I've no idea where *he* is.

CAPT. MORGAN: You've lost him?

FRUTE: Never found him.

CAPT. MORGAN: Don't torment me, I beg of you. What are you trying to blurt out?

FRUTE: Up till now, no other man has put in an appearance.

CAPT. MORGAN: Up till now . . .?

FRUTE: Your wife, and my observations but confirm the opinion I first formed of her, appears to be an honest and indeed an innocent woman.

[*Pause.*]

CAPT. MORGAN (*horrified*): How can that be possible?

FRUTE: They exist.

CAPT. MORGAN: But she . . . she wanted the separation. She broke up our marriage.

FRUTE: Some time ago.

CAPT. MORGAN: Nothing very innocent about that.

FRUTE: There may have been no . . . other man.

[*Pause.*]

CAPT. MORGAN (*incredulous*): You're not suggesting —that she simply took a dislike to me. . . .

FRUTE: One wouldn't credit it.

CAPT. MORGAN: But I'm well liked. Even some women have rather liked me.

FRUTE: Well, now. . . .

CAPT. MORGAN: Look me steadily in the eye. What could she have found not to love about me? Great Scott, it's not logical. There must have been a seducer.

FRUTE: That's our hope.

CAPT. MORGAN: You do give me then, that small glimmer of hope?

FRUTE: If we continue our investigations. . . .

CAPT. MORGAN: Continue them please. Continue them like a good little fellow.

FRUTE: You'll permit a word of advice?

CAPT. MORGAN: Yes.

FRUTE: Take a train. First class as your rank is entitled. Go home. Leave this job to the experts. All that the human eye can see of your wife is under observation.

[*Frute exits.*]

CAPT. MORGAN: Very well . . . I'll take your advice . . . news of her infidelity would be a great comfort. . . . (*His voice trails off as he shouts after Frute.*)

[*Fade out.*]

[*When the lights fade in the lawyer is finishing a meal at the dining table. Mrs. Morgan has just finished waiting on him. Frute enters the serving room behind the screen.*]

LAWYER: No doubt you are competent at your work, madam, and you may call it anti-feminism, but I want the waiter to bring me my bill.

[*Mrs. Morgan shrugs her shoulders and goes behind the screen into the serving room. There, Frute is singing to himself.*]

FRUTE (*singing*):
> " We always come back for . . .
> There's no place like home " . . . .

MRS. MORGAN: You sound happy. Business going well?

FRUTE: There comes a time, Mrs. Morgan, in any business, when you have to control the customer—and when it comes there's a battle of wills, a moment of courage and puff—you get what you want. And all without stooping to a single untruth—a touch of deception.

MRS. MORGAN: There's a gentleman alone in there. He says he wants the waiter to bring him his bill.

FRUTE: A gentleman?

[*He peers through the screen then says aghast:*]

Mrs. Morgan, I think I'm off.

LAWYER: Waiter!

MRS. MORGAN: Too late. He's spied you. . . .

LAWYER: Waiter!

FRUTE (*faintly*): Coming, coming at once, sir.

[*Frute goes round the screen and stands by the dining table. Mrs. Morgan exits.*]

LAWYER: Well, Frute. It appears that I have winkled you out at last.

FRUTE: We can't talk here, sir—if I may suggest. (*He writes the bill hurriedly and puts it on the table.*)

LAWYER: I will be brief, while the lady in question is

out of the room. For me, you must realise, this is
but one of a thousand cases.

FRUTE: Of course. I realise that, sir.

LAWYER: Good. Now listen to me, Frute.

FRUTE: Yes, sir.

LAWYER: This case is not going well.

FRUTE: No, sir.

LAWYER: The client is not satisfied.

FRUTE: I realise that . . . very painful for him.

LAWYER: And painful for you, Frute.

FRUTE: Yes, sir.

LAWYER: Now time is money, and you have wasted
enough of both. I have backed you so far—now I
expect results—I expect some tangible fact to
emerge. . . .

FRUTE: But sir—how can it?

LAWYER: I know nothing of your methods of going
to work.

FRUTE: No, sir.

LAWYER: Nor do I want to know. We trained men,
professional men, have our code, Frute. We have
our ethics. Within the strict frame of proper conduct
we have woven the beautiful patterns of law. You
are outside all that—

FRUTE (*humbly*): Yes, sir.

LAWYER: You, Frute, have passed no examination.
You have won no fine-engraved certificates—
not only are you beyond reach of professional
qualifications, honourable standards or disciplinary
bodies, you are even remote from any normal test
of human decency. What honourable man, I ask you,
would invite a private detective to take tea with his
wife or play with his children? The absurdity of the
idea strikes you at once, does it not?

FRUTE: I suppose it does.

LAWYER: Very well, Frute. What you do, how you

go about your calling is happily no concern of mine. Only don't attempt to impose on your repulsive trade the standards which are the monopoly of the decently employed citizen. You have no right to do that, Frute.

FRUTE: I suppose not, sir.

LAWYER: Bear that well in mind. And if I don't get a result in this case I shall feel unable to recommend you in future. I don't imagine, at your age, you feel particularly suited for other work? I don't fancy they'd keep you on as a waiter if I told. . . .

FRUTE: I understand. . . .

LAWYER: Very good. Let there be no unpleasantness. I do not care for unpleasantness. In your own line you may still be a success. But remember, I impress on you, what your particular line has to be. There *is* a pale, Frute, and *you* are beyond it.

[*The lawyer leaves money for the bill and exits. Frute goes back into the serving room, sits on the table and mops his brow. Mrs. Morgan enters to him.*]

MRS. MORGAN (*solicitous*): Mr. Frute, you look quite ill.

[*Pause while Frute gasps and gulps.*]

What is it, have you been trying to do too much?

FRUTE: Perhaps that's what it is.

MRS. MORGAN: Cheer up. " Time off " again on Thursday.

FRUTE: Time off?

MRS. MORGAN: Makes a change for us, anyway.

FRUTE: You won't be . . . meeting anyone?

MRS. MORGAN (*patiently*): No, Mr. Frute. You know that, now don't you?

FRUTE: Yes, I know. (*pause*) Probably you won't even speak to another man?

MRS. MORGAN: Probably not.

FRUTE: Let alone have tea with one.

MRS. MORGAN: No. . . .

FRUTE: Or talk in an animated manner. . . .

MRS. MORGAN: Not with Gladys.

FRUTE: Or be spotted arm in arm on the promenade.

MRS. MORGAN (*laughing slightly*): Certainly not.

FRUTE: Then it's hopeless.

MRS. MORGAN: Unlikely.

FRUTE: Unless. . . .

[*Pause.*]

MRS. MORGAN: What did you say?

FRUTE: Unless. You would consider . . . you would allow. . . .

MRS. MORGAN: Allow?

FRUTE: Allow me to be your escort for the " time off "?

MRS. MORGAN: Oh, Mr. Frute. What a long time it's taken you to ask.

[*They exit together. The lights fade.*]

[*Fade in background. Mrs. Morgan and Frute enter in their hats and coats and stand looking out at the beach. There is a sound of distant children's voices singing:*]

"Eternal father, strong to save,
Whose hand doth bound the restless waves,
Who bidst the mighty ocean deep. . . ."

MRS. MORGAN: The children's service, on the beach.

FRUTE: I can see now. There's a harmonium on the wet sand.

MRS. MORGAN: The Salvation Army organise it. Something to keep the kiddies warm.

FRUTE: On a summer holiday—not very festive. . . .

MRS. MORGAN (*singing*): "For those in peril *on* the sea."

FRUTE: What's that?

MRS. MORGAN: I was just thinking. . . .

FRUTE: What?

MRS. MORGAN: That day—when you thought there was peril at sea, remember—and how quick you were to get out on the pier, to strip off. . . .

FRUTE: No, Mrs. Morgan. I'm no hero. All the same I hope you'll remember me kindly. When I move on.

[*They go to the shelter and sit down together.*]

MRS. MORGAN: You're leaving us? Nothing wrong?

FRUTE: Purely business.

MRS. MORGAN: Oh. I'm sorry.

FRUTE: I'm sorry too, Mrs. Morgan.

MRS. MORGAN: Waitering for you's only a sideline, isn't it, really?

FRUTE: That—is so.

MRS. MORGAN: What's this other business of yours— I mean the one where you control the customer?

FRUTE: Alas, Mrs. Morgan, I don't control him any more.

MRS. MORGAN: But what is that business exactly?

FRUTE: Private. . . .

MRS. MORGAN: Oh well. I never meant to butt in.

FRUTE: A confidential. . . .

MRS. MORGAN: I quite understand. Really, you

know the old "Stag at Bay" won't seem the same without you.

FRUTE: Won't it, Mrs. Morgan?

MRS. MORGAN: It never seemed exactly a homely place, not before you came.

FRUTE: Not?

MRS. MORGAN: But now, when I look around it, I fall to imagining. I mean, suppose that "Stag at Bay" were our home. It's a dream. . . .

FRUTE: A bit of a nightmare. (*Laughing*.)

MRS. MORGAN: You're laughing. I may be stupid. But you and I, Mr. Frute, we've no other home—so if I sometimes think, that was ours. . . .

FRUTE: Ours, Mrs. Morgan?

MRS. MORGAN (*almost chanting*): The twenty bottles of sauce on the tables—our bottles of sauce, the twenty cruets—our cruets. All those antlers—our antlers. And the visitors and staff—all our friends and relations.

FRUTE: Even Gladys?

MRS. MORGAN: Poor Gladys. She's a decent sort really.

FRUTE: Yes. A decent sort.

[*Pause.*]

MRS. MORGAN: It's a funny thing. All these years and I had no one even to send a postcard to. Once I even bought a postcard and sent it to *him*, I was that lonely.

FRUTE: To *him*?

MRS. MORGAN: The Captain. Now that showed I was feeling a lack.

FRUTE: What happened?

MRS. MORGAN: Oh, he never even answered it. Took no notice, really.

FRUTE: You can't be sure. It may have meant a lot to him.

MRS. MORGAN: I doubt that. (*Chanting again.*) The palm tree in the lounge, our palm tree.

FRUTE: It's no good going on, Mrs. Morgan. I just don't fit into the pattern of family life.

MRS. MORGAN: Not fit in?

FRUTE: I'm outside it somehow. I've had it all explained. . . .

MRS. MORGAN: Whatever can you mean?

FRUTE: You may find it difficult to understand.

MRS. MORGAN: Yes.

FRUTE: But what I'm doing for you—well I only hope it will make you feel more free, when. . . .

MRS. MORGAN: "When". . . .

FRUTE (*with a rush*): When a man of decent quali- fications does come along—as we hope and believe he must.

[*Pause.*]

MRS. MORGAN: After you're gone. . . . I can send you a postcard?

FRUTE: Certainly Mrs. Morgan—and to tell you the truth. . . . I'm really glad it was me you went out with today. I shouldn't have liked it to have been anyone else, not today, know what I mean?

MRS. MORGAN: Can't say I do.

FRUTE: Time will show, Mrs. Morgan. It is, I want you to understand, just my peculiar line.

MRS. MORGAN: I'm sure you mean no harm.

FRUTE: I don't, really I don't.

MRS. MORGAN: Come on then, we'll miss the picture. I must say it'll be nice having someone to talk to in the pictures, when they play the organ and the lights go up and all the couples round you are caught so friendly.

FRUTE: It makes a difference, having someone to talk to.

MRS. MORGAN: The pictures don't drag so. Come on. We'll miss the love picture. Do you like love pictures, Mr. Frute?

FRUTE: Up to now I've always preferred detection. Of course, detective work. . . .

MRS. MORGAN: Yes?

FRUTE: It's more concerned with love than many people might think. . . .

[*The lights fade as they exit together. Cinema organ music is heard for a moment, then the lights fade in on serving room.*]

[*Mrs. Morgan and Mr. Frute come in in their outdoor coats.*]

MRS. MORGAN (*yawns*): Best " time off " I ever had.

FRUTE: Me too.

MRS. MORGAN: I'm climbing up to the home from home.

FRUTE: Which is?

MRS. MORGAN: Room 51. Right up the stairs. Just next door to the water tank. You must be tired.

FRUTE: Not really. And I've still a little writing to do.

MRS. MORGAN: Get you something?

FRUTE: No thanks. And thank you, Mrs. Morgan— thank you for everything.

[*Pause. As she goes.*]

MRS. MORGAN: Don't work too hard at that old writing now. . . .

[*She gives him a lingering, solicitous look and goes out of the door. Frute sits down at the serving table, takes out his notebook and pencil, and begins to wrestle with his conscience.*]

FRUTE (*sighs. Pauses. Whistles the first bar of " No Place Like Home " sighs again*): What did he say? No professional standards. No disciplinary bodies. No normal test of human decency. . . . Beyond the pale . . . (*sighs*) He's right, Frute. You know he's right. (*sighs*) It's a useful job after all. After all, someone's got to do it. After all, we can't all choose. (*determined*) Go on Frute, put pencil to paper. (*regretful*) Oh, you never even gave her back her pencil. . . . (*whispering*) Get on with it, man, and—make it lively reading. . . . Make it artistic. Write it, like you always wanted it to happen. . . .

[*Frute exits.*]

[*Fade in lights on lawyer's office. Lawyer and Captain have entered quietly during Frute's last speech. The lawyer is just finishing reading Frute's last report.*]

LAWYER: "And after their departure from the Pix Picture Palace, where it is not suggested misconduct took place, the evening ended with the gentleman in question escorting Mrs. Morgan to her ' home from home ' as she so phrases it, room number 51, at the top of the stairs, next door to the water tank."

[*The lawyer looks at Captain Morgan in great and silent satisfaction. Then he opens a drawer of the desk, brings out a sherry decanter and two glasses, fills them and motions his client to a glass. They raise glasses solemnly to each other and drink.*]

CAPT. MORGAN: Frute's been brilliant. Just brilliant. Quite a first-class brain he must have under that quaint old hat of his. For a moment you know, I'd misjudged him.

LAWYER: I always told you, I think, that Frute was a perfectly sound little worker.

CAPT. MORGAN: To pull the solution out of the bag when everyone has despaired of him. Bang in the tradition, wouldn't you agree, of the great detective brains of all time?

LAWYER: Our organisation, I think, must take a little of the credit.

CAPT. MORGAN: Good heavens, yes. I didn't imply. . . .

LAWYER: Frute was merely content to fulfil his somewhat sordid function. He obeyed instructions. Few of us can do more.

CAPT. MORGAN: Indeed no. And now it's definite. There's another man. I'm safe. I feel well-liked—I feel surrounded with affection. Oh, the difference Frute has made to me. And Mrs. Morgan?

LAWYER: Will receive her Divorce Petition, based on her matrimonial misconduct, in a sealed envelope and by A.R. Registered Post.

CAPT. MORGAN (*thinking*): Registered Post, eh? Serve her right if it is by Registered Post. Great Scott, I'd like to see her face when she opens that. . . . Registered Post did you say?

[*They have finished their drinks and the lawyer, nodding, ushers the Captain firmly out of the office. As they exit, fade in light on the serving room.*]

[*Mrs. Morgan enters with a suitcase. She puts the case down and looks round regretfully. Frute enters with his possessions in a paper parcel. They are both in outdoor clothes. They look at each other in surprise.*]

MRS. MORGAN: You're leaving?

FRUTE: My work's over. But you. . . .

MRS. MORGAN: I had this. (*Pulls paper from her overcoat.*)

FRUTE: Oh, yes. That. . . .

MRS. MORGAN: It seems I've done misconduct.

FRUTE: Well, you see. . . .

MRS. MORGAN (*reading*): "On Thursday, the 12th day of September, at the 'Stag at Bay' Hotel, Cold Sands." I'd better leave. I can't get the old Stag involved in that sort of thing. It's got enough to depress it already.

FRUTE: Very considerate.

MRS. MORGAN (*reading*): "With a man unknown. . . ." (*Looks up.*) Mr. Frute, there was no unknown man! You were with me all the time. You can say. . . . Why, whatever's the matter . . . ?

FRUTE: Mrs. Morgan, I feel ashamed. I think even I . . . even I'm entitled to feel ashamed.

MRS. MORGAN: Of course you are, Mr. Frute, if you really want to.

FRUTE: I feel really terrible. But there was no harm to me. When I first felt drawn to this class of work. . . .

MRS. MORGAN: Poor Mr. Frute. You've had a terrible shock.

FRUTE: It was only a young boy's spirit of adventure. At the home when the other boys were out playing on the asphalt, I was locked. . . . I'm boring you.

MRS. MORGAN (*completely bewildered*): No, Mr. Frute. You were locked apparently. . . .

FRUTE: In the lavatory by the old boiler room.

Reading. How the muffled woman came to Baker Street, how the secret papers got into the breakfast dish. How the rose came from Ruritania.

MRS. MORGAN: Enthralled?

FRUTE: Even at that age I knew the risks I was running. I had to be skilled with the foils, sudden with a loaded ash plant, able to sit for long hours in silence in a darkened room and only a mulatto breathing for company. . . .

MRS. MORGAN: Sounds creepy.

FRUTE: Not woman's work, I can assure you. Then, when I left the home I found the opening at last. I became a private. . . .

MRS. MORGAN: Yes, Mr. Frute?

FRUTE: Detective. And of course I became—beyond the pale—as the expression is.

MRS. MORGAN: In what way, Mr. Frute?

FRUTE: Nice people, Mrs. Morgan, don't know many private detectives.

MRS. MORGAN: Their loss, Mr. Frute.

FRUTE: Kind of you to say so, but . . . what I'm trying to get out is—it was in the course of my work that we. . . .

MRS. MORGAN: Yes?

FRUTE: Met.

MRS. MORGAN: Met, Mr. Frute?

FRUTE: I was employed by your husband—to keep an eye on you.

MRS. MORGAN (*very quiet and thoughtful*): So you. . . .

FRUTE: Yes. And I wrote the report that led to that terrible accusation. Oh, Mrs. Morgan—I took a terrible liberty with the truth. . . .

MRS. MORGAN: Yes, Mr. Frute.

FRUTE: It was all—wishful thinking.

MRS. MORGAN: Wishful?

FRUTE (*very agitated*): But I'll deny it all. I'll say it

was all a lie. I'll clear your name. You've been so kind. . . . Oh, Mrs. Morgan. I'll put it right.

MRS. MORGAN (*thoughtful*): Mr. Frute. If you don't deny it. If you go to Court and give clear oath evidence of my . . . misconduct?

FRUTE: I couldn't!

MRS. MORGAN: But if you could. . . .

FRUTE: It would be a terrible deception, of the Judge, your husband, you . . . even me. . . .

MRS. MORGAN: Yes. And I'd be free?

FRUTE: I expect so. Yes.

MRS. MORGAN: To marry again?

FRUTE: If you wanted to.

MRS. MORGAN: I do want to.

[*Pause.*]

FRUTE: To a particular gentleman?

MRS. MORGAN: To a man who never expected anyone to like him. To someone such as. . . .

FRUTE: Yes?

MRS. MORGAN: You, Mr. Frute.

[*Pause.*]

FRUTE: I don't know what to say. . . . If you *would* consider life as Mrs. Frute.

MRS. MORGAN: Give that clear, oath evidence! Give them the worst of me, Mr. Frute! Give them misconduct *and* adultery!

FRUTE: Mrs. Morgan, I will. You're a truly remarkable woman, quite outstanding. I loved you from the moment I first had you under observation.

MRS. MORGAN: And we'll be happy, Mr. Frute.

FRUTE: I'll give up my profession.

MRS. MORGAN: Why ever?

FRUTE: To a lady of your stamp . . . it's no doubt distasteful.

MRS. MORGAN: It's not distasteful at all. It seems a very useful profession.

FRUTE: Another pair of eyes is often a help.

MRS. MORGAN: I'd be proud to help, Mr. Frute. And we might manage a small home?

FRUTE: No doubt of it. Shall we be off, Mrs. Morgan?

MRS. MORGAN: Mrs. Morgan? Mrs. Morgan—as was. (*triumphantly*) Mrs. Frute, to you.

[*They leave the serving room and they are last seen walking arm in arm across the back of the stage as the Curtain slowly falls.*]

A Selected List of Evergreen Books